I0162131

The Inn Album by Robert Browning

Robert Browning is one of the most significant Victorian Poets and, of course, English Poetry.

Much of his reputation is based upon his mastery of the dramatic monologue although his talents encompassed verse plays and even a well-regarded essay on Shelley during a long and prolific career.

He was born on May 7th, 1812 in Walmouth, London. Much of his education was home based and Browning was an eclectic and studious student, learning several languages and much else across a myriad of subjects, interests and passions.

Browning's early career began promisingly. The fragment from his intended long poem Pauline brought him to the attention of Dante Gabriel Rossetti, and was followed by Paracelsus, which was praised by both William Wordsworth and Charles Dickens. In 1840 the difficult Sordello, which was seen as willfully obscure, brought his career almost to a standstill.

Despite these artistic and professional difficulties his personal life was about to become immensely fulfilling. He began a relationship with, and then married, the older and better known Elizabeth Barrett. This new foundation served to energise his writings, his life and his career.

During their time in Italy they both wrote much of their best work. With her untimely death in 1861 he returned to London and thereafter began several further major projects.

The collection Dramatis Personae (1864) and the book-length epic poem The Ring and the Book (1868-69) were published and well received; his reputation as a venerated English poet now assured.

Robert Browning died in Venice on December 12th, 1889.

Index of Contents

The story told in this poem was suggested to Browning, but not followed in all its details, by an adventure of Lord De Ros, a friend of Wellington's and mentioned frequently by Greville in his Memoirs. The circumstances of De Ros's villainy were much talked of in London at the time of their occurrence, just before the middle of this century.

"That oblong book 's the Album; hand it here!
Exactly! page on page of gratitude
For breakfast, dinner, supper, and the view!
I praise these poets, they leave margin-space;

Each stanza seems to gather skirts around,
And primly, trimly, keep the foot's confine,
Modest and maidlike; lubber prose o'ersprawls
And straddling stops the path from left to right.
Since I want space to do my cipher-work,
Which poem spares a corner? What comes first?
'Hail, calm acclivity, salubrious spot!'
(Open the window, we burn daylight, boy!)
Or see—succincter beauty, brief and bold—'
If a fellow can dine On rump-steaks and port wine,
He needs not despair Of dining well here'—
'Here!' I myself could find a better rhyme!
That bard 's a Browning; he neglects the form:
But ah, the sense, ye gods, the weighty sense!
Still, I prefer this classic. Ay, throw wide!
I 'll quench the bits of candle yet unburnt.
A minute's fresh air, then to cipher-work!
Three little columns hold the whole account:
Ecarté, after which Blind Hookey, then
Cutting-the-Pack, five hundred pounds the cut.
'T is easy reckoning: I have lost, I think."

Two personages occupy this room
Shabby-genteel, that 's parlor to the inn
Perched on a view-commanding eminence;
—Inn which may be a veritable house
Where somebody once lived and pleased good taste
Till tourists found his coigne of vantage out,
And fingered blunt the individual mark,
And vulgarized things comfortably smooth.
On a sprig-pattern-papered wall there brays
Complaint to sky Sir Edwin's dripping stag;
His couchant coast-guard creature corresponds;
They face the Huguenot and Light o' the World.
Grim o'er the mirror on the mantelpiece,
Varnished and coffined, Salmo ferox glares,
—Possibly at the List of Wines which, framed
And glazed, hangs somewhat prominent on peg.

So much describes the stuffy little room—
Vulgar flat smooth respectability:
Not so the burst of landscape surging in,
Sunrise and all, as he who of the pair
Is, plain enough, the younger personage
Draws sharp the shrieking curtain, sends aloft
The sash, spreads wide and fastens back to wall
Shutter and shutter, shows you England's best.
He leans into a living glory-bath

Of air and light where seems to float and move
The wooded watered country, hill and dale
And steel-bright thread of stream, a-smoke with mist,
A-sparkle with May morning, diamond drift
O' the sun-touched dew. Except the red-roofed patch
Of half a dozen dwellings that, crept close
For hillside shelter, make the village-clump,
This inn is perched above to dominate—
Except such sign of human neighborhood,
"And this surmised rather than sensible"
There 's nothing to disturb absolute peace,
The reign of English nature—which means art
And civilized existence. Wildness' self
Is just the cultured triumph. Presently
Deep solitude, be sure, reveals a Place
That knows the right way to defend itself:
Silence hems round a burning spot of life.
Now, where a Place burns, must a village brood,
And where a village broods, an inn should boast—
Close and convenient: here you have them both.
This inn, the Something-arms—the family's—
(Don't trouble Guillim: heralds leave out half!)
Is dear to lovers of the picturesque,
And epics have been planned here; but who plan
Take holy orders and find work to do.
Painters are more productive, stop a week,
Declare the prospect quite a Corot,—ay,
For tender sentiment,—themselves incline
Rather to handsweep large and liberal;
Then go, but not without success achieved
—Haply some pencil-drawing, oak or beech,
Ferns at the base and ivies up the bole,
On this a slug, on that a butterfly.
Nay, he who hooked the salmo pendent here,
Also exhibited, this same May-month,
"Foxgloves: a study"—so inspires the scene,
The air, which now the younger personage
Inflates him with till lungs o'erfraught are fain
Sigh forth a satisfaction might bestir
Even those tufts of tree-tops to the South
I' the distance where the green dies off to gray,
Which, easy of conjecture, front the Place;
He eyes them, elbows wide, each hand to cheek.
His fellow, the much older—either say
A youngish-old man or man oldish-young—
Sits at the table: wicks are noisome-deep
In wax, to detriment of plated ware;
Above—piled, strewn—is store of playing-cards,

Counters and all that 's proper for a game.
He sets down, rubs out figures in the book,
Adds and subtracts, puts back here, carries there,
Until the summed-up satisfaction stands
Apparent, and he pauses o'er the work:
Soothes what of brain was busy under brow,
By passage of the hard palm, curing so
Wrinkle and crowfoot for a second's space;
Then lays down book and laughs out. No mistake,
Such the sum-total—ask Colenso else!

Roused by which laugh, the other turns, laughs too—
The youth, the good strong fellow, rough perhaps.

"Well, what 's the damage—three, or four, or five?
How many figures in a row? Hand here!
Come now, there's one expense all yours not mine—
Scribbling the people's Album over, leaf
The first and foremost too! You think, perhaps,
They 'll only charge you for a brand-new book
Nor estimate the literary loss?
Wait till the small account comes! 'To one night's
Lodging,' for—'beds' they can't say,—'pound or so;
Dinner, Apollinaris,—what they please,
Attendance not included;' last looms large
'Defacement of our Album, late enriched
With'—let 's see what! Here, at the window, though!
Ay, breathe the morning and forgive your luck!
Fine enough country for a fool like me
To own, as next month I suppose I shall!
Eh? True fool's-fortune! so console yourself,
Let 's see, however—hand the book, I say!
Well, you 've improved the classic by romance.
Queer reading! Verse with parenthetic prose—
'Hail, calm acclivity, salubrious spot!'
(Three-two fives) 'life how profitably spent'
(Five-naught, five-nine fives) 'yonder humble cot,'
(More and more naughts and fives) 'in mild content;
And did my feelings find the natural vent
In friendship and in love, how blest my lot!'
Then follow the dread figures—five! 'Content?'
That 's appetite! Are you content as he—
Simpkin the sonneteer? Ten thousand pounds
Give point to his effusion—by so much
Leave me the richer and the poorer you
After our night's play; who 's content the most,
If, you, or Simpkin?"
So the polished snob.

The elder man, refinement every inch
From brow to boot-end, quietly replies:

"Simpkin 's no name I know. I had my whim."

"Ay, had you! And such things make friendship thick.
Intimates, I may boast we were; henceforth,
Friends—shall it not be?—who discard reserve,
Use plain words, put each dot upon each i,
Till death us twain do part? The bargain 's struck!
Old fellow, if you fancy—(to begin—)
I failed to penetrate your scheme last week,
You wrong your poor disciple. Oh, no airs!
Because you happen to be twice my age
And twenty times my master, must perforce
No blink of daylight struggle through the web
There 's no unwinding? You entoil my legs,
And welcome, for I like it: blind me,—no!
A very pretty piece of shuttle-work
Was that—your mere chance question at the club—
'Do you go anywhere this Whitsuntide?
I'm off for Paris, there 's the Opera—there 's
The Salon, there 's a china-sale,—beside
Chantilly; and, for good companionship,
There 's Such-and-such and So-and-so. Suppose
We start together?' 'No such holiday!'
I told you: 'Paris and the rest be hanged!
Why plague me who am pledged to home-delights?
I 'm the engaged now; through whose fault but yours?
On duty. As you well know. Don't I drowse
The week away down with the Aunt and Niece?
No help: it 's leisure, loneliness, and love.
'Wish I could take you; but fame travels fast,—
A man of much newspaper-paragraph,
You scare domestic circles; and beside
Would not you like your lot, that second taste
Of nature and approval of the grounds!
You might walk early or lie late, so shirk
Week-day devotions: but stay Sunday o'er,
And morning church is obligatory:
No mundane garb permissible, or dread
The butler's privileged monition! ~No~!
Pack off to Paris, nor wipe tear away!'
Whereon how artlessly the happy flash
Followed, by inspiration! "Tell you what—
Let 's turn their flank, try things on t' other side!
Inns for my money! Liberty 's the life!
We 'll lie in hiding: there 's the crow-nest nook,

The tourist's joy, the Inn they rave about,
Inn that 's out—out of sight and out of mind
And out of mischief to all four of us—
Aunt and niece, you and me. At night arrive;
At morn, find time for just a Pisgah-view
Of my friend's Land of Promise; then depart.
And while I'm whizzing onward by first train,
Bound for our own place (since my Brother sulks
And says I shun him like the plague) yourself—
Why, you have stepped thence, start from platform, gay
Despite the sleepless journey,—love lends wings,—
Hug aunt and niece who, none the wiser, wait
The faithful advent! Eh?' 'With all my heart,'
Said I to you; said I to mine own self:
'Does he believe I fail to comprehend
He wants just one more final friendly snack
At friend's exchequer ere friend runs to earth,
Marries, renounces yielding friends such sport?'
And did I spoil sport, pull face grim,—nay, grave?
Your pupil does you better credit! No!
I parleyed with my pass-book,—rubbed my pair
At the big balance in my banker's hands,—
Folded a check cigar-case-shape,—just wants
Filling and signing,—and took train, resolved
To execute myself with decency
And let you win—if not Ten thousand quite,
Something by way of wind-up-farewell burst
Of firework-nosegay! Where 's your fortune fled?
Or is not fortune constant after all?
You lose ten thousand pounds: had I lost half
Or half that, I should bite my lips, I think.
You man of marble! Strut and stretch my best
On tiptoe, I shall never reach your height.
How does the loss feel! Just one lesson more!"

The more refined man smiles a frown away.

"The lesson shall be—only boys like you
Put such a question at the present stage.
I had a ball lodge in my shoulder once,
And, full five minutes, never guessed the fact;
Next day, I felt decidedly: and still,
At twelve years' distance, when I lift my arm
A twinge reminds me of the surgeon's probe.
Ask me, this day month, how I feel my luck!
And meantime please to stop impertinence,
For—don't I know its object? All this chaff
Covers the corn, this preface leads to speech,

This boy stands forth a hero. 'There, my lord!
Our play was true play, fun not earnest! I
Empty your purse, inside out, while my poke
Bulges to bursting? You can badly spare
A doit, confess now, Duke though brother be!
While I 'm gold-daubed so thickly, spangles drop
And show my father's warehouse-apron: pshaw!
Enough! We 've had a palpitating night!
Good morning! Breakfast and forget our dreams!
My mouth 's shut, mind! I tell nor man nor mouse.'
There, see! He don't deny it! Thanks, my boy!
Hero and welcome—only, not on me
Make trial of your 'prentice-hand! Enough!
We 've played, I 've lost and owe ten thousand pounds,
Whereof I muster, at the moment,—well,
What 's for the bill here and the back to town.
Still, I 've my little character to keep;
You may expect your money at month's end."

The young man at the window turns round quick—
A clumsy giant handsome creature; grasps
In his large red the little lean white hand
Of the other, looks him in the sallow face.

"I say now—is it right to so mistake
A fellow, force him in mere self-defence
To spout like Mister Mild Acclivity
In album-language? You know well enough
Whether I like you—like 's no album-word,
Anyhow: point me to one soul beside
In the wide world I care one straw about!
I first set eyes on you a year ago;
Since when you 've done me good—I 'll stick to it—
More than I got in the whole twenty-five
That make my life up, Oxford years and all—
Throw in the three I fooled away abroad,
Seeing myself and nobody more sage
Until I met you, and you made me man
Such as the sort is and the fates allow.
I do think, since we two kept company,
I 've learnt to know a little—all through you!
It 's nature if I like you. Taunt away!
As if I need you teaching me my place—
The snob I am, the Duke your brother is,
When just the good you did was—teaching me
My own trade, how a snob and millionaire
May lead his life and let the Duke's alone,
Clap wings, free jackdaw, on his steeple-perch,

Burnish his black to gold in sun and air,
Nor pick up stray plumes, strive to match in strut
Regular peacocks who can't fly an inch
Over the courtyard-paling. Head and heart
(That 's album-style) are older than you know,
For all your knowledge: boy, perhaps—ay, boy
Had his adventure, just as he were man—
His ball-experience in the shoulder-blade,
His bit of life-long ache to recognize,
Although he bears it cheerily about,
Because you came and clapped him on the back,
Advised him 'Walk and wear the aching off!'
Why, I was minded to sit down for life
Just in Dalmatia, build a seaside tower
High on a rock, and so expend my days
Pursuing chemistry or botany
Or, very like, astronomy because
I noticed stars shone when I passed the place.
Letting my cash accumulate the while
In England—to lay out in lump at last
As Ruskin should direct me! All or some
Of which should I have done or tried to do,
And preciously repented, one fine day,
Had you discovered Timon, climbed his rock
And scaled his tower, some ten years thence, suppose,
And coaxed his story from him! Don't I see
The pair conversing! It 's a novel writ
Already, I 'll be bound,—our dialogue!
'What?' cried the elder and yet youthful man—
So did the eye flash 'neath the lordly front,
And the imposing presence swell with scorn,
As the haught high-bred bearing and dispose
Contrasted with his interlocutor
The flabby low-born who, of bulk before,
Had steadily increased, one stone per week,
Since his abstention from horse-exercise:—
'What? you, as rich as Rothschild, left, you say
London the very year you came of age,
Because your father manufactured goods—
Commission-agent hight of Manchester—
Partly, and partly through a baby case
Of disappointment I've pumped out at last—
And here you spend life 's prime in gaining flesh
And giving science one more asteroid?'
Brief, my dear fellow, you instructed me,
At Alfred's and not Istria! proved a snob
May turn a million to account although
His brother be no Duke, and see good days

Without the girl he lost and some one gained.
The end is, after one year's tutelage,
Having, by your help, touched society,
Polo, Tent-pegging, Hurlingham, the Rink—
I leave all these delights, by your advice,
And marry my young pretty cousin here
Whose place, whose oaks ancestral you behold.
(Her father was in partnership with mine—
Does not his purchase look a pedigree?)
My million will be tails and tassels smart
To this plump-bodied kite, this house and land
Which, set a-soaring, pulls me, soft as sleep,
Along life's pleasant meadow,—arm left free
To lock a friend's in,—whose, but yours, old boy?
Arm in arm glide we over rough and smooth,
While hand, to pocket held, saves cash from cards.
Now, if you don't esteem ten thousand pounds
(—Which I shall probably discover snug
Hid somewhere in the column-corner capped
With 'Credit,' based on 'Balance,'—which, I swear,
By this time next month I shall quite forget
Whether I lost or won—ten thousand pounds,
Which at this instant I would give ... let 's see,
For Galopin—nay, for that Gainsborough
Sir Richard won't sell, and, if bought by me,
Would get my glance and praise some twice a year,—)
Well, if you don't esteem that price dirt-cheap
For teaching me Dalmatia was mistake—
Why then, my last illusion-bubble breaks,
My one discovered phœnix proves a goose,
My cleverest of all companions—oh,
Was worth nor ten pence nor ten thousand pounds!
Come! Be yourself again! So endeth here
The morning's lesson! Never while life lasts
Do I touch card again. To breakfast now!
To bed—I can't say, since you needs must start
For station early—oh, the down-train still,
First plan and best plan—townward trip be hanged!
You 're due at your big brother's—pay that debt,
Then owe me not a farthing! Order eggs—
And who knows but there 's trout obtainable?"

The fine man looks wellnigh malignant: then—

"Sir, please subdue your manner! Debts are debts:
I pay mine—debts of this sort—certainly.
What do I care how you regard your gains,
Want them or want them not? The thing I want

Is—not to have a story circulate
From club to club—how, bent on clearing out,
Young So-and-so, young So-and-so cleaned me,
Then set the empty kennel flush again,
Ignored advantage and forgave his friend—
For why? There was no wringing blood from stone!
Oh, don't be savage! You would hold your tongue,
Bite it in two, as man may; but those small
Hours in the smoking-room, when instance apt
Rises to tongue's root, tingles on to tip,
And the thinned company consists of six
Capital well-known fellows one may trust!
Next week, it 's in the 'World.' No, thank you much.
I owe ten thousand pounds: I 'll pay them!"

"Now,—
This becomes funny. You 've made friends with me:
I can't help knowing of the ways and means!
Or stay! they say your brother closets up
Correggio's long lost Leda: if he means
To give you that, and if you give it me" ...

"I polished snob off to aristocrat?
You compliment me! father's apron still
Sticks out from son's court-vesture; still silk purse
Roughs finger with some bristle sow-ear-born!
Well, neither I nor you mean harm at heart!
I owe you and shall pay you: which premised,
Why should what follows sound like flattery?
The fact is—you do compliment too much
Your humble master, as I own I am;
You owe me no such thanks as you protest.
The polisher needs precious stone no less
Than precious stone needs polisher: believe
I struck no tint from out you but I found
Snug lying first 'neath surface hairbreadth-deep!
Beside, I liked the exercise: with skill
Goes love to show skill for skill's sake. You see,
I 'm old and understand things: too absurd
It were you pitched and tossed away your life,
As diamond were Scotch-pebble! all the more,
That I myself misused a stone of price.
Born and bred clever—people used to say
Clever as most men, if not something more—
Yet here I stand a failure, cut awry
Or left opaque,—no brilliant named and known.
Whate'er my inner stuff, my outside 's blank;
I 'm nobody—or rather, look that same—

I 'm—who I am—and know it; but I hold
What in my hand out for the world to see?
What ministry, what mission, or what book
—I 'll say, book even? Not a sign of these!
I began—laughing—'All these when I like!'
I end with—well, you 've hit it!—'This boy's check
For just as many thousands as he he 'll spare!'
The first—I could, and would not; your spare cash
I would, and could not: have no scruple, pray,
But, as I hoped to pocket yours, pouch mine
—When you are able!"

"Which is—when to be?
I 've heard, great characters require a fall
Of fortune to show greatness by uprise:
They touch the ground to jollily rebound,
Add to the Album! Let a fellow share
Your secret of superiority!
I know, my banker makes the money breed
Money; I eat and sleep, he simply takes
The dividends and cuts the coupons off,
Sells out, buys in, keeps doubling, tripling cash,
While I do nothing but receive and spend.
But you, spontaneous generator, hatch
A wind-egg; cluck, and forth struts Capital
As Interest to me from egg of gold.
I am grown curious: pay me by all means!
How will you make the money?"

"Mind your own—
Not my affair. Enough: or money, or
Money's worth, as the case may be, expect
Ere month's end,—keep but patient for a month!
Who 's for a stroll to station? Ten 's the time;
Your man, with my things, follow in the trap;
At stoppage of the down-train, play the arrived
On platform, and you 'll show the due fatigue
Of the night-journey,—not much sleep,—perhaps,
Your thoughts were on before you—yes, indeed,
You join them, being happily awake
With thought's sole object as she smiling sits
At breakfast-table. I shall dodge meantime
In and out station-precinct, wile away
The hour till up my engine pants and smokes.
No doubt, she goes to fetch you. Never fear!
She gets no glance at me, who shame such saints!"

II

So, they ring bell, give orders, pay, depart
Amid profuse acknowledgment from host
Who well knows what may bring the younger back.
They light cigar, descend in twenty steps
The "calm acclivity," inhale—beyond
Tobacco's balm—the better smoke of turf
And wood fire,—cottages at cookery
I' the morning,—reach the main road straightening on
'Twixt wood and wood, two black walls full of night
Slow to disperse, though mists thin fast before
The advancing foot, and leave the flint-dust fine
Each speck with its fire-sparkle. Presently
The road's end with the sky's beginning mix
In one magnificence of glare, due East,
So high the sun rides,—May 's the merry month.

They slacken pace: the younger stops abrupt,
Discards cigar, looks his friend full in face.

"All right; the station comes in view at end;
Five minutes from the beech-clump, there you are!
I say: let 's halt, let 's borrow yonder gate
Of its two magpies, sit and have a talk!
Do let a fellow speak a moment! More
I think about and less I like the thing—
No, you must let me! Now, be good for once!
Ten thousand pounds be done for, dead and damned!
We played for love, not hate: yes, hate! I hate
Thinking you beg or borrow or reduce
To strychnine some poor devil of a lord
Licked at Unlimited Loo. I had the cash
To lose—you knew that!—lose and none the less
Whistle to-morrow: it 's not every chap
Affords to take his punishment so well!
Now, don't be angry with a friend whose fault
Is that he thinks—upon my soul, I do—
Your head the best head going. Oh, one sees
Names in the newspaper—great This, great That,
Gladstone, Carlyle, the Laureate:—much I care!
Others have their opinion, I keep mine:
Which means—by right you ought to have the things
I want a head for. Here 's a pretty place,
My cousin's place, and presently my place,
Not yours! I 'll tell you how it strikes a man.
My cousin 's fond of music and of course
Plays the piano (it won't be for long!)

A brand-new bore she calls a 'semi-grand'
Rosewood and pearl, that blocks the drawing-room,
And cost no end of money. Twice a week
Down comes Herr Somebody and seats himself,
Sets to work teaching—with his teeth on edge—
I 've watched the rascal. 'Does he play first-rate?'
I ask: 'I rather think so,' answers she—
'He's What's-his-Name!'—'Why give you lessons then?'—
'I pay three guineas and the train beside.'—
'This instrument, has he one such at home?'—
'He? Has to practise on a table-top,
When he can't hire the proper thing.'—'I see!
You 've the piano, he the skill, and God
The distribution of such gifts.' So here:
After your teaching, I shall sit and strum
Polkas on this piano of a Place
You 'd make resound with 'Rule Britannia'!"

"Thanks!
I don't say but this pretty cousin's place,
Appendaged with your million, tempts my hand
As key-board I might touch with some effect."

"Then, why not have obtained the like? House, land,
Money, are things obtainable, you see,
By clever head-work: ask my father else!
You, who teach me, why not have learned, yourself?
Played like Herr Somebody with power to thump
And flourish and the rest, not bend demure
Pointing out blunders—'Sharp, not natural!
Permit me—on the black key use the thumb!'
There 's some fatality, I 'm sure! You say
'Marry the cousin, that's your proper move!'
And I do use the thumb and hit the sharp:
You should have listened to your own head's hint,
As I to you! The puzzle 's past my power,
How you have managed—with such stuff, such means—
Not to be rich nor great nor happy man:
Of which three good things where 's a sign at all?
Just look at Dizzy! Come,—what tripped your heels?
Instruct a goose that boasts wings and can't fly!
I wager I have guessed it!—never found
The old solution of the riddle fail!
'Who was the woman?' I don't ask, but—'Where
I' the path of life stood she who tripped you?'"

"Goose
You truly are! I own to fifty years.

Why don't I interpose and cut out—you?
Compete with five-and-twenty? Age, my boy!"

"Old man, no nonsense!—even to a boy
That 's ripe at least for rationality
Rapped into him, as maybe mine was, once!
I 've had my small adventure lesson me
Over the knuckles!—likely, I forget
The sort of figure youth cuts now and then,
Competing with old shoulders but young head
Despite the fifty grizzling years!"

"Aha?
Then that means—just the bullet in the blade
Which brought Dalmatia on the brain,—that, too,
Came of a fatal creature? Can't pretend
Now for the first time to surmise as much!
Make a clean breast! Recount! a secret 's safe
'Twixt you, me, and the gate-post!"

"—Can't pretend,
Neither, to never have surmised your wish!
It 's no use,—case of unextracted ball—
Winces at finger-touching. Let things be!"

"Ah, if you love your love still! I hate mine."

"I can't hate."

"I won't teach you; and won't tell
You, therefore, what you please to ask of me:
As if I, also, may not have my ache!"

"My sort of ache? No, no! and yet—perhaps!
All comes of thinking you superior still.
But live and learn! I say! Time 's up! Good jump!
You old, indeed! I fancy there 's a cut
Across the wood, a grass-path: shall we try?
It 's venturesome, however!"

"Stop, my boy!
Don't think I 'm stingy of experience! Life
—It 's like this wood we leave. Should you and I
Go wandering about there, though the gaps
We went in and came out by were opposed
As the two poles still, somehow, all the same
By nightfall we should probably have chanced
On much the same main points of interest—

Both of us measured girth, of mossy trunk,
Stript ivy from its strangled prey, clapped hands
At squirrel, sent a fir-cone after crow,
And so forth,—never mind what time betwixt.
So in our lives; allow I entered mine
Another way than you: 't is possible
I ended just by knocking head against
That plaguy low-hung branch yourself began
By getting bump from; as at last you too
May stumble o'er that stump which first of all
Bade me walk circumspectly. Head and feet
Are vulnerable both, and I, foot-sure,
Forgot that ducking down saves brow from bruise.
I, early old, played young man four years since
And failed confoundedly: so, hate alike
Failure and who caused failure,—curse her cant!"

"Oh, I see! You, though somewhat past the prime,
Were taken with a rosebud beauty! Ah—
But how should chits distinguish? She admired
Your marvel of a mind, I 'll undertake!
But as to body ... nay, I mean ... that is,
When years have told on face and figure" ...

"Thanks,
Mister Sufficiently-Instructed! Such
No doubt was bound to be the consequence
To suit your self-complacency: she liked
My head enough, but loved some heart beneath
Some head with plenty of brown hair a-top
After my young friend's fashion! What becomes
Of that fine speech you made a minute since
About the man of middle age you found
A formidable peer at twenty-one?
So much for your mock-modesty! and yet
I back your first against this second sprout
Of observation, insight, what you please.
My middle age, Sir, had too much success!
It 's odd: my case occurred four years ago—
I finished just while you commenced that turn
I' the wood of life that takes us to the wealth
Of honeysuckle, heaped for who can reach.
Now, I don't boast: it 's bad style, and beside,
The feat proves easier than it looks: I plucked
Full many a flower unnamed in that bouquet
(Mostly of peonies and poppies, though!)
Good-nature sticks into my buttonhole.
Therefore it was with nose in want of snuff

Rather than Ess or Psidium, that I chanced
On what—so far from 'rosebud beauty' ... Well—
She 's dead: at least you never heard her name;
She was no courtly creature, had nor birth
Nor breeding—mere fine-lady-breeding; but
Oh, such a wonder of a woman! Grand
As a Greek statue! Stick fine clothes on that,
Style that a Duchess or a Queen,—you know,
Artists would make an outcry: all the more,
That she had just a statue's sleepy grace
Which broods o'er its own beauty. Nay, her fault
(Don't laugh!) was just perfection: for suppose
Only the little flaw, and I had peeped
Inside it, learned what soul inside was like.
At Rome some tourist raised the grit beneath
A Venus' forehead with his whittling-knife—
I wish—now—I had played that brute, brought blood
To surface from the depths I fancied chalk!
As it was, her mere face surprised so much
That I stopped short there, struck on heap, as stares
The cockney stranger at a certain bust
With drooped eyes,—she 's the thing I have in mind,—
Down at my Brother's. All sufficient prize—
Such outside! Now,—confound me for a prig!—
Who cares? I 'll make a clean breast once for all!
Beside, you 've heard the gossip. My life long
I 've been a woman-liker,—liking means
Loving and so on. There 's a lengthy list
By this time I shall have to answer for—
So say the good folk: and they don't guess half—
For the worst is, let once collecting-itch
Possess you, and, with perspicacity,
Keeps growing such a greediness that theft
Follows at no long distance,—there 's the fact!
I knew that on my Leporello-list
Might figure this, that, and the other name
Of feminine desirability,
But if I happened to desire inscribe,
Along with these, the only Beautiful—
Here was the unique specimen to snatch
Or now or never. 'Beautiful' I said—
'Beautiful' say in cold blood,—boiling then
To tune of 'Haste, secure whatever the cost
This rarity, die in the act, be damned,
So you complete collection, crown your list!'
It seemed as though the whole world, once aroused
By the first notice of such wonder's birth,
Would break bounds to contest my prize with me

The first discoverer, should she but emerge
From that safe den of darkness where she dozed
Till I stole in, that country-parsonage
Where, country-parson's daughter, motherless,
Brotherless, sisterless, for eighteen years
She had been vegetating lily-like.
Her father was my brother's tutor, got
The living that way: him I chanced to see—
Her I saw—her the world would grow one eye
To see, I felt no sort of doubt at all!
'Secure her!' cried the devil: 'afterward
Arrange for the disposal of the prize!'
The devil's doing! yet I seem to think—
Now, when all 's done,—think with 'a head reposed'
In French phrase—hope I think I meant to do
All requisite for such a rarity
When I should be at leisure, have due time
To learn requirement. But in evil day—
Bless me, at week's end, long as any year,
The father must begin, 'Young Somebody,
Much recommended—for I break a rule—
Comes here to read, next Long Vacation.'—'Young!'
That did it. Had the epithet been 'rich,'
'Noble,' 'a genius,' even 'handsome,'—but
—'Young'!"

"I say—just a word! I want to know—
You are not married?"

"I?"

"Nor ever were?"

"Never! Why?"

"Oh, then—never mind! Go on!
I had a reason for the question."

"Come,—
You could not be the young man?"

"No, indeed!
Certainly—if you never married her!"

"That I did not: and there 's the curse, you 'll see!
Nay, all of it 's one curse, my life's mistake
Which nourished with manure that 's warranted
To make the plant bear wisdom, blew out full

In folly beyond fieldflower-foolishness!
The lies I used to tell my womankind!
Knowing they disbelieved me all the time
Though they required my lies, their decent due,
This woman—not so much believed, I 'll say,
As just anticipated from my mouth:
Since being true, devoted, constant—she
Found constancy, devotion, truth, the plain
And easy commonplace of character.
No mock-heroics but seemed natural
To her who underneath the face, I knew
Was fairness' self, possessed a heart, I judged
Must correspond in folly just as far
Beyond the common,—and a mind to match,—
Not made to puzzle conjurers like me
Who, therein, proved the fool who fronts you, Sir,
And begs leave to cut short the ugly rest!
'Trust me!' I said: she trusted. 'Marry me!'
Or rather, 'We are married: when, the rite?'
That brought on the collector's next-day qualm
At counting acquisition's cost. There lay
My marvel, there my purse more light by much
Because of its late lie-expenditure:
Ill-judged such moment to make fresh demand—
To cage as well as catch my rarity!
So, I began explaining. At first word
Outbroke the horror. 'Then, my truths were lies!'
I tell you, such an outbreak, such new strange
All-unsuspected revelation—soul
As supernaturally grand as face
Was fair beyond example—that at once
Either I lost—or, if it please you, found
My senses,—stammered somehow—'Jest! and now,
Earnest! Forget all else but—heart has loved,
Does love, shall love you ever! take the hand!'
Not she! no marriage for superb disdain,
Contempt incarnate!"

"Yes, it 's different,—
It 's only like in being four years since.
I see now!"

"Well, what did disdain do next,
Think you?"

"That's past me: did not marry you!—-
That 's the main thing I care for, I suppose.
Turned nun, or what?"

"Why, married in a month
Some parson, some smug crop-haired smooth-chinned sort
Of curate-creature, I suspect,—dived down,
Down, deeper still, and came up somewhere else—
I don't know where—I 've not tried much to know,—
In short, she 's happy: what the clodpoles call
'Countrified' with a vengeance! leads the life
Respectable and all that drives you mad:
Still—where, I don't know, and that 's best for both."

"Well, that she did not like you, I conceive.
But why should you hate her, I want to know?"

"My good young friend,—because or her or else
Malicious Providence I have to hate.
For, what I tell you proved the turning-point
Of my whole life and fortune toward success
Or failure. If I drown, I lay the fault
Much on myself who caught at reed not rope,
But more on reed which, with a packthread's pith,
Had buoyed me till the minute's cramp could thaw
And I strike out afresh and so be saved.
It 's easy saying—I had sunk before,
Disqualified myself by idle days
And busy nights, long since, from holding hard
On cable, even, had fate cast me such!
You boys don't know how many times men fail
Perforce o' the little to succeed i' the large,
Husband their strength, let slip the petty prey,
Collect the whole power for the final pounce!
My fault was the mistaking man's main prize
For intermediate boy's diversion; clap
Of boyish hands here frightened game away
Which, once gone, goes forever. Oh, at first
I took the anger easily, nor much
Minded the anguish—having learned that storms
Subside, and teapot-tempests are akin.
Time would arrange things, mend whate'er might be
Somewhat amiss; precipitation, eh?
Reason and rhyme prompt—reparation! Tiffs
End properly in marriage and a dance!
I said 'We 'll marry, make the past a blank'—
And never was such damnable mistake!
That interview, that laying bare my soul,
As it was first, so was it last chance—one
And only. Did I write? Back letter came
Unopened as it went. Inexorable

She fled, I don't know where, consoled herself
With the smug curate-creature: chop and change!
Sure am I, when she told her shaveling all
His Magdalen's adventure, tears were shed,
Forgiveness evangelically shown,
'Loose hair and lifted eye,'—as some one says.
And now, he 's worshipped for his pains, the sneak!"

"Well, but your turning-point of life,—what 's here
To hinder you contesting Finsbury
With Orton, next election? I don't see" ...

"Not you! But I see. Slowly, surely, creeps
Day by day o'er me the conviction—here
Was life's prize grasped at, gained, and then let go!
—That with her—maybe, for her—I had felt
Ice in me melt, grow steam, drive to effect
Any or all the fancies sluggish here
I' the head that needs the hand she would not take
And I shall never lift now, Lo, your wood—
Its turnings which I likened life to! Well,—
There she stands, ending every avenue,
Her visionary presence on each goal
I might have gained had we kept side by side!
Still string nerve and strike foot? Her frown forbids:
The steam congeals once more: I 'm old again!
Therefore I hate myself—but how much worse
Do not I hate who would not understand,
Let me repair things—no, but sent a-slide
My folly falteringly, stumblingly
Down, down, and deeper down until I drop
Upon—the need of your ten thousand pounds
And consequently loss of mine! I lose
Character, cash, nay, common-sense itself
Recounting such a lengthy cock-and-bull
Adventure, lose my temper in the act" ...

"And lose beside,—if I may supplement
The list of losses,—train and ten-o'clock!
Hark, pant and puff, there travels the swart sign!
So much the better! You 're my captive now!
I 'm glad you trust a fellow: friends grow thick
This way—that 's twice said; we were thickish, though,
Even last night, and, ere night comes again,
I prophesy good luck to both of us!
For see now!—back to 'balmy eminence'
Or 'calm acclivity' or what 's the word!
Bestow you there an hour, concoct at ease

A sonnet for the Album, while I put
Bold face on, best foot forward, make for house,
March in to aunt and niece, and tell the truth—
(Even white-lying goes against my taste
After your little story.) Oh, the niece
Is rationality itself! The aunt—
If she 's amenable to reason too—
Why, you stopped short to pay her due respect,
And let the Duke wait (I 'll work well the Duke).
If she grows gracious, I return for you;
If thunder 's in the air, why—bear your doom,
Dine on rump-steaks and port, and shake the dust
Of aunty from your shoes as off you go
By evening-train, nor give the thing a thought
How you shall pay me—that 's as sure as fate.
Old fellow! Off with you, face left about!
Yonder 's the path I have to pad. You see,
I 'm in good spirits, God knows why! Perhaps
Because the woman did not marry you
—Who look so hard at me,—and have the right,
One must be fair and own."

The two stand still
Under an oak.

"Look here!" resumes the youth.
"I never quite knew how I came to like
You—so much—whom I ought not court at all:
Nor how you had a leaning just to me
Who am assuredly not worth your pains.
For there must needs be plenty such as you
Somewhere about,—although I can't say where,—
Able and willing to teach all you know;
While—how can you have missed a score like me
With money and no wit, precisely each
A pupil for your purpose, were it—ease
Fool's poke of tutor's honorarium-fee?
And yet, howe'er it came about, I felt
At once my master: you as prompt descried
Your man, warrant, so was bargain struck.
Now, these same lines of liking, loving, run
Sometimes so close together they converge—
Life's great adventures—you know what I mean—
In people. Do you know, as you advanced,
It got to be uncommonly like fact
We two had fallen in with—liked and loved
Just the same woman in our different ways?
I began life—poor groundling as I prove—

and ambitious to fly high: why not?
There 's something in 'Don Quixote' to the point,
My shrewd old father used to quote and praise—
'Am I born man?' asks Sancho; 'being man,
By possibility I may be Pope!'
So, Pope I meant to make myself, by step
And step, whereof the first should be to find
A perfect woman; and I tell you this—
If what I fixed on, in the order due
Of undertakings, as next step, had first
Of all disposed itself to suit my tread,
And I had been, the day I came of age,
Returned at head of poll for Westminster
—Nay, and moreover summoned by the Queen
At week's end, when my maiden-speech bore fruit,
To form and head a Tory ministry—
It would not have seemed stranger, no, nor been
More strange to me, as now I estimate,
Than what did happen—sober truth, no dream.
I saw my wonder of a woman,—laugh,
I'm past that!—in Commemoration-week.
A plenty have I seen since, fair and foul,—
With eyes, too, helped by your sagacious wink;
But one to match that marvel—no least trace,
Least touch of kinship and community!
The end was—I did somehow state the fact,
Did, with no matter what imperfect words,
One way or other give to understand
That woman, soul and body were her slave
Would she but take, but try them—any test
Of will, and some poor test of power beside:
So did the strings within my brain grow tense
And capable of ... hang similitudes!
She answered kindly but beyond appeal.
'No sort of hope for me, who came too late.
She was another's. Love went—mine to her,
Hers just as loyally to some one else.'
Of course! I might expect it! Nature's law—
Given the peerless woman, certainly
Somewhere shall be the peerless man to match!
I acquiesced at once, submitted me
In something of a stupor, went my way.
I fancy there had been some talk before
Of somebody—her father or the like—
To coach me in the holidays,—that's how
I came to get the sight and speech of her,—
But I had sense enough to break off sharp,
Save both of us the pain."

"Quite right there!"

"Eh?
Quite wrong, it happens! Now comes worst of all!
Yes, I did sulk aloof and let alone
The lovers—I disturb the angel-mates?"

"Seraph paired off with cherub!"

"Thank you! While
I never plucked up courage to inquire
Who he was, even,—certain-sure of this,
That nobody I knew of had blue wings
And wore a star-crown as he needs must do,—
Some little lady,—plainish, pock-marked girl,—
Finds out my secret in my woeful face,
Comes up to me at the Apollo Ball,
And pityingly pours her wine and oil
This way into the wound: 'Dear f-f-friend,
Why waste affection thus on—must I say,
A somewhat worthless object? Who's her choice—
Irrevocable as deliberate—
Out of the wide world? I shall name no names—
But there's a person in society,
Who, blessed with rank and talent, has grown gray
In idleness and sin of every sort
Except hypocrisy: he's thrice her age,
A byword for 'successes with the sex'
As the French say—and, as we ought to say.
Consummately a liar and a rogue,
Since—show me where's the woman won without
The help of this one lie which she believes—
That—never mind how things have come to pass,
And let who loves have loved a thousand times—
All the same he now loves her only, loves
Her ever! if by 'won' you just mean 'sold,'
That's quite another compact. Well, this scamp,
Continuing descent from bad to worse,
Must leave his fine and fashionable prey
(Who—fathered, brothered, husbanded,—are hedged
About with thorny danger) and apply
His arts to this poor country ignorance
Who sees forthwith in the first rag of man
Her model hero! Why continue waste
On such a woman treasures of a heart
Would yet find solace,—yes, my f-f-friend—
In some congenial—fiddle-diddle-dee?'"

"Pray, is the pleasant gentleman described
Exact the portrait which my 'f-f-friends'
Recognize as so like? 'Tis evident
You half surmised the sweet original
Could be no other than myself, just now!
Your stop and start were flattering!"

"Of course
Caricature's allowed for in a sketch!
The longish nose becomes a foot in length,
The swarthy cheek gets copper-colored,—still,
Prominent beak and dark-hued skin are facts:
And 'parson's daughter'—'young man coachable'—
'Elderly party'—'four years since'—were facts
To fasten on, a moment! Marriage, though—
That made the difference, I hope."

"All right!
I never married; wish I had—and then
Unwish it: people kill their wives, sometimes!
I hate my mistress, but I'm murder-free.
In your case, where's the grievance? You came last,
The earlier bird picked up the worm. Suppose
You, in the glory of your twenty-one,
Had happened to precede myself! 'tis odds
But this gigantic juvenility,
This offering of a big arm's bony hand—
I'd rather shake than feel shake me, I know—
Had moved my dainty mistress to admire
An altogether new Ideal—deem
Idolatry less due to life's decline
Productive of experience, powers mature
By dint of usage, the made man—no boy
That's all to make! I was the earlier bird—
And what I found, I let fall; what you missed,
Who is the fool that blames you for?"

"Myself—
For nothing, everything! For finding out
She, whom I worshipped, was a worshipper
In turn of ... but why stir up settled mud?
She married him—the fifty-years-old rake—
How you have teased the talk from me! At last
My secret's told you. I inquired no more,
Nay, stopped ears when informants unshut mouth;
Enough that she and he live, deuce take where,
Married and happy, or else miserable—

It's 'Cut-the-pack;' she turned up ace or knave,
And I left Oxford, England, dug my hole
Out in Dalmatia, till you drew me thence
Badger-like,—'Back to London' was the word—
'Do things, a many, there, you fancy hard,
I'll undertake are easy!'—the advice.
I took it, had my twelvemonth's fling with you—
(Little hand holding large hand pretty tight
For all its delicacy—eh, my lord?)
Until when, t'other day, I got a turn
Somehow and gave up tired: and 'Rest!' bade you,
'Marry your cousin, double your estate,
And take your ease by all means!' So, I loll
On this the springy sofa, mine next month—
Or should loll, but that you must needs beat rough
The very down you spread me out so smooth.
I wish this confidence were still to make!
Ten thousand pounds? You owe me twice the sum
For stirring up the black depths! There's repose
Or, at least, silence when misfortune seems
All that one has to bear; but folly—yes,
Folly, it all was! Fool to be so meek,
So humble,—such a coward rather say!
Fool, to adore the adorer of a fool!
Not to have faced him, tried (a useful hint)
My big and bony, here, against the bunch
Of lily-colored five with signet-ring,
Most like, for little-finger's sole defence—
Much as you flaunt the blazon there! I grind
My teeth, that bite my very heart, to think—
To know I might have made that woman mine
But for the folly of the coward—know—
Or what's the good of my apprenticeship
This twelvemonth to a master in the art?
Mine—had she been mine—just one moment mine
For honor, for dishonor—anyhow,
So that my life, instead of stagnant ... Well,
You've poked and proved stagnation is not sleep—
Hang you!"

"Hang you for an ungrateful goose!
All this means—I who since I knew you first
Have helped you to conceit yourself this cock
O' the dunghill with all hens to pick and choose—
Ought to have helped you when shell first was chipped
By chick that wanted prompting 'Use the spur!'
While I was elsewhere putting mine to use.
As well might I blame you who kept aloof,

Seeing you could not guess I was alive,
Never advised me 'Do as I have done—
Reverence such a jewel as your luck
Has scratched up to enrich unworthiness!'
As your behavior was, should mine have been,
—Faults which we both, too late, are sorry for:
Opposite ages, each with its mistake:
'If youth but would—if age but could,' you know.
Don't let us quarrel! Come, we're—young and old—
Neither so badly off. Go you your way,
Cut to the Cousin! I'll to Inn, await
The issue of diplomacy with Aunt,
And wait my hour on 'calm acclivity'
In rumination manifold—perhaps
About ten thousand pounds I have to pay!"

III

Now, as the elder lights the fresh cigar
Conducive to resource, and saunteringly
Betakes him to the left-hand backward path,—
While, much sedate, the younger strides away
To right and makes for—islanded in lawn
And edged with shrubbery—the brilliant bit
Of Barry's building that's the Place,—a pair
Of women, at this nick of time, one young,
One very young, are ushered with due pomp
Into the same Inn-parlor—"disengaged
Entirely now!" the obsequious landlord smiles,
"Since the late occupants—whereof but one
Was quite a stranger"—(smile enforced by bow)
"Left, a full two hours since, to catch the train,
Probably for the stranger's sake!" (Bow, smile,
And backing out from door soft-closed behind.)

Woman and girl, the two, alone inside,
Begin their talk: the girl, with sparkling eyes—
"Oh, I forewent him purposely! but you,
Who joined at—journeyed from the Junction here—
I wonder how he failed your notice. Few
Stop at our station: fellow-passengers
Assuredly you were—I saw indeed
His servant, therefore he arrived all right.
I wanted, you know why, to have you safe
Inside here first of all, so dodged about
The dark end of the platform; that's his way—
To swing from station straight to avenue

And stride the half a mile for exercise.
I fancied you might notice the huge boy.
He soon gets o'er the distance; at the house
He'll hear I went to meet him and have missed;
He'll wait. No minute of the hour's too much
Meantime for our preliminary talk:
First word of which must be—oh, good beyond
Expression of all goodness—you to come!"

The elder, the superb one, answers slow.

"There was no helping that. You called for me,
Cried, rather: and my old heart answered you.
Still, thank me! since the effort breaks a vow—
At least, a promise to myself."

"I know!
How selfish get you happy folk to be!
If I should love my husband, must I needs
Sacrifice straightway all the world to him,
As you do? Must I never dare leave house
On this dread Arctic expedition, out
And in again, six mortal hours, though you,
You even, my own friend forevermore,
Adjure me—fast your friend till rude love pushed
Poor friendship from her vantage—just to grant
The quarter of a whole day's company
And counsel? This makes counsel so much more
Need and necessity. For here's my block
Of stumbling: in the face of happiness
So absolute, fear chills me. If such change
In heart be but love's easy consequence,
Do I love? If to marry mean—let go
All I now live for, should my marriage be?"

The other never once has ceased to gaze
On the great elm-tree in the open, posed
Placidly full in front, smooth bole, broad branch,
And leafage, one green plenitude of May.
The gathered thought runs into speech at last.

"O you exceeding beauty, bosomful
Of lights and shades, murmurs and silences,
Sun-warmth, dew-coolness,—squirrel, bee and bird,
High, higher, highest, till the blue proclaims
'Leave earth, there's nothing better till next step
Heavenward!'—so, off flies what has wings to help!"

And henceforth they alternate. Says the girl—

"That's saved then: marriage spares the early taste."

"Four years now, since my eye took note of tree!"

"If I had seen no other tree but this
My life long, while yourself came straight, you said,
From tree which overstretched you and was just
One fairy tent with pitcher-leaves that held
Wine, and a flowery wealth of suns and moons,
And magic fruits whereon the angels feed—
I looking out of window on a tree
Like yonder—otherwise well-known, much-liked,
Yet just an English ordinary elm—
What marvel if you cured me of conceit
My elm's bird-bee-and-squirrel tenantry
Was quite the proud possession I supposed?
And there is evidence you tell me true.
The fairy marriage-tree reports itself
Good guardian of the perfect face and form,
Fruits of four years' protection! Married friend,
You are more beautiful than ever!"

"Yes:
I think that likely. I could well dispense
With all thought fair in feature, mine or no,
Leave but enough of face to know me by—
With all found fresh in youth except such strength
As lets a life-long labor earn repose
Death sells at just that price, they say; and so,
Possibly, what I care not for, I keep."

"How you must know he loves you! Chill, before,
Fear sinks to freezing. Could I sacrifice—
Assured my lover simply loves my soul—
One nose-breadth of fair feature? No, indeed!
Your own love" ...

"The preliminary hour—
Don't waste it!"

"But I can't begin at once!
The angel's self that comes to hear me speak
Drives away all the care about the speech.
What an angelic mystery you are—
Now—that is certain! when I knew you first,
No break of halo and no bud of wing!

I thought I knew you, saw you, round and through,
Like a glass ball; suddenly, four years since,
You vanished, how and whither? Mystery!
Wherefore? No mystery at all: you loved,
Were loved again, and left the world of course:
Who would not? Lapped four years in fairyland,
Out comes, by no less wonderful a chance,
The changeling, touched athwart her trellised bliss
Of blush-rose bower by just the old friend's voice
That's now struck dumb at her own potency.
I talk of my small fortunes? Tell me yours
Rather! The fool I ever was—I am,
You see that: the true friend you ever had,
You have, you also recognize. Perhaps,
Giving you all the love of all my heart,
Nature, that's niggard in me, has denied
The after-birth of love there 's some one claims,
—This huge boy, swinging up the avenue;
And I want counsel: is defect in me,
Or him who has no right to raise the love?
My cousin asks my hand: he's young enough,
Handsome,—my maid thinks,—manly's more the word:
He asked my leave to 'drop' the elm-tree there,
Some morning before breakfast. Gentleness
Goes with the strength, of course. He's honest too,
Limpidly truthful. For ability—
All's in the rough yet. His first taste of life
Seems to have somehow gone against the tongue:
He travelled, tried things—came back, tried still more—
He says he 's sick of all. He 's fond of me
After a certain careless-earnest way
I like: the iron 's crude,—no polished steel
Somebody forged before me. I am rich—
That 's not the reason, he 's far richer: no,
Nor is it that he thinks me pretty,—frank
Undoubtedly on that point! He saw once
The pink of face-perfection—oh, not you—
Content yourself, my beauty!—for she proved
So thoroughly a cheat, his charmer ... nay,
He runs into extremes, I 'll say at once,
Lest you say! Well, I understand he wants
Some one to serve, something to do: and both
Requisites so abound in me and mine
That here 's the obstacle which stops consent—
The smoothness is too smooth, and I mistrust
The unseen cat beneath the counterpane.
Therefore I thought—'Would she but judge for me,
Who, judging for herself succeeded so!'

Do I love him, does he love me, do both
Mistake for knowledge—easy ignorance?
Appeal to its proficient in each art!
I got rough-smooth through a piano-piece,
Rattled away last week till tutor came,
Heard me to end, then grunted 'Ach, mein Gott!
Sagen Sie "easy"? Every note is wrong!
All thumped mit wrist—we 'll trouble fingers now.
The Fräulein will please roll up Raff again
And exercise at Czerny for one month!'
Am I to roll up cousin, exercise
At Trollope's novels for one month? Pronounce!"

"Now, place each in the right position first,
Adviser and advised one! I perhaps
Am three—nay, four years older; am, beside,
A wife: advantages—to balance which,
You have a full fresh joyous sense of life
That finds you out life's fit food everywhere,
Detects enjoyment where I, slow and dull,
Fumble at fault. Already, these four years,
Your merest glimpses at the world without
Have shown you more than ever met my gaze;
And now, by joyance you inspire joy,—learn
While you profess to teach, and teach, although
Avowedly a learner. I am dazed
Like any owl by sunshine which just sets
The sparrow preening plumage! Here 's to spy
—Your cousin! You have scanned him all your life,
Little or much; I never saw his face.
You have determined on a marriage—used
Deliberation therefore—I 'll believe
No otherwise, with opportunity
For judgment so abounding! Here stand I—
Summoned to give my sentence, for a whim,
(Well, at first cloud-fleck thrown athwart your blue,)
Judge what is strangeness' self to me,—say 'Wed!'
Or 'Wed not!' whom you promise I shall judge
Presently, at propitious lunch-time, just
While he carves chicken! Sends he leg for wing?
That revelation into character
And conduct must suffice me! Quite as well
Consult with yonder solitary crow
That eyes us from your elm-top!"

"Still the same!
Do you remember, at the library
We saw together somewhere, those two books

Somebody said were notice-worthy? One
Lay wide on table, sprawled its painted leaves
For all the world's inspection; shut on shelf
Reclined the other volume, closed, clasped, locked—
Clear to be let alone. Which page had we
Preferred the turning over of? You were,
Are, ever will be the locked lady, hold
Inside you secrets written,—soul absorbed,
My ink upon your blotting-paper. I—
What trace of you have I to show in turn?
Delicate secrets! No one juvenile
Ever essayed at croquet and performed
Superiorly but I confided you
The sort of hat he wore and hair it held.
While you? One day a calm note comes by post—
'I am just married, you may like to hear.'
Most men would hate you, or they ought; we love
What we fear,—I do! 'Cold' I shall expect
My cousin calls you. I—dislike not him,
But (if I comprehend what loving means)
Love you immeasurably more—more—more
Than even he who, loving you his wife,
Would turn up nose at who impertinent,
Frivolous, forward—loves that excellence
Of all the earth he bows in worship to!
And who 's this paragon of privilege?
Simply a country parson: his the charm
That worked the miracle! Oh, too absurd—
But that you stand before me as you stand!
Such beauty does prove something, everything!
Beauty 's the prize-flower which dispenses eye
From peering into what has nourished root—
Dew or manure: the plant best knows its place.
Enough, from teaching youth and tending age
And hearing sermons,—haply writing tracts,—
From such strange love-besprinkled compost, lo,
Out blows this triumph! Therefore love 's the soil
Plants find or fail of. You, with wit to find,
Exercise wit on the old friend's behalf,
Keep me from failure! Scan and scrutinize
This cousin! Surely he 's as worth your pains
To study as my elm-tree, crow and all,
You still keep staring at. I read your thoughts."

"At last?"

"At first! 'Would, tree, a-top of thee
I wingèd were, like crow perched moveless there,

And so could straightway soar, escape this bore,
Back to my nest where broods whom I love best—
The parson o'er his parish—garish—rarish,'—
Oh, I could bring the rhyme in if I tried:
The Album here inspires me! Quite apart
From lyrical expression, have I read
The stare aright, and sings not soul just so?"

"Or rather so? 'Cool comfortable elm
That men make coffins out of,—none for me
At thy expense, so thou permit I glide
Under thy ferny feet, and there sleep, sleep,
Nor dread awaking though in heaven itself!'"

The younger looks with face struck sudden white.
The elder answers its inquiry.

"Dear,
You are a guesser, not a 'clairvoyante.'
I 'll so far open you the locked and shelved
Volume, my soul, that you desire to see,
As let you profit by the title-page"—

"Paradise Lost?"

"Inferno!—All which comes
Of tempting me to break my vow. Stop here!
Friend, whom I love the best in the whole world,
Come at your call, be sure that I will do
All your requirement—see and say my mind.
It may be that by sad apprenticeship
I have a keener sense: I 'll task the same.
Only indulge me,—here let sight and speech
Happen,—this Inn is neutral ground, you know!
I cannot visit the old house and home,
Encounter the old sociality
Abjured forever. Peril quite enough
In even this first—last, I pray it prove—
Renunciation of my solitude!
Back, you, to house and cousin! Leave me here,
Who want no entertainment, carry still
My occupation with me. While I watch
The shadow inching round those ferny feet,
Tell him 'A school-friend wants a word with me
Up at the inn: time, tide, and train won't wait:
I must go see her—on and off again—
You 'll keep me company?' Ten minutes' talk,
With you in presence, ten more afterward

With who, alone, convoys me station-bound,
And I see clearly—and say honestly
To-morrow: pen shall play tongue's part, you know.
Go—quick! for I have made our hand-in-hand
Return impossible. So scared you look,—
If cousin does not greet you with 'What ghost
Has crossed your path?' I set him down obtuse."

And after one more look, with face still white,
The younger does go, while the elder stands
Occupied by the elm at window there.

IV

Occupied by the elm; and, as its shade
Has crept clock-hand-wise till it ticks at fern
Five inches further to the South,—the door
Opens abruptly, some one enters sharp,
The elder man returned to wait the youth:
Never observes the room's new occupant,
Throws hat on table, stoops quick, elbow propped
Over the Album wide there, bends down brow
A cogitative minute, whistles shrill,
Then,—with a cheery-hopeless laugh-and-lose
Air of defiance to fate visibly
Casting the toils about him—mouths once more
'Hail, calm acclivity, salubrious spot!'
Then clasps-to cover, sends book spinning off
T' other side table, looks up, starts erect
Full-face with her who—roused from that abstruse
Question 'Will next tick tip the fern or no?'—
Fronts him as fully.

All her languor breaks,
Away withers at once the weariness
From the black-blooded brow, anger and hate
Convulse. Speech follows slowlier, but at last—

"You here! I felt, I knew it would befall!
Knew, by some subtle undivinable
Trick of the trickster, I should, silly-sooth,
Late or soon, somehow be allured to leave
Safe hiding and come take of him arrears,
My torment due on four years' respite! Time
To pluck the bird's healed, breast of down o'er wound!
Have your success! Be satisfied this sole
Seeing you has undone all heaven could do

These four years, puts me back to you and hell!
What will next trick be, next success? No doubt
When I shall think to glide into the grave,
There will you wait disguised as beckoning Death,
And catch and capture me forevermore!
But, God, though I am nothing, be thou all!
Contest him for me! Strive, for he is strong!"

Already his surprise dies palely out
In laugh of acquiescing impotence.
He neither gasps nor hisses: calm and plain—

"I also felt and knew—but otherwise!
You out of hand and sight and care of me
These four years, whom I felt, knew, all the while ...
Oh, it 's no superstition! It 's a gift
O' the gamester that he snuffs the unseen powers
Which help or harm him. Well I knew what lurked,
Lay perdue paralyzing me,—drugged, drowsed
And damnified my soul and body both!
Down and down, see where you have dragged me to,
You and your malice! I was, four years since,
—Well, a poor creature! I became a knave.
I squandered my own pence: I plump my purse
With other people's pounds. I practised play
Because I liked it: play turns labor now
Because there 's profit also in the sport.
I gamed with men of equal age and craft:
I steal here with a boy as green as grass
Whom I have tightened hold on slow and sure
This long while, just to bring about to-day
When the boy beats me hollow, buries me
In ruin who was sure to beggar him.
Oh, time indeed I should look up and laugh
'Surely she closes on me!' Here you stand!"

And stand she does: while volubility,
With him, keeps on the increase, for his tongue
After long locking-up is loosed for once.

"Certain the taunt is happy!" he resumes:
"So, I it was allured you—only I
—I, and none other—to this spectacle—
Your triumph, my despair—you woman-fiend
That front me! Well, I have my wish, then! See
The low wide brow oppressed by sweeps of hair
Darker and darker as they coil and swathe
The crowned corpse-wanness whence the eyes burn black,

Not asleep now! not pin-points dwarfed beneath
Either great bridging eyebrow—poor blank beads—
Babies, I 've pleased to pity in my time:
How they protrude and glow immense with hate!
The long-triumphant nose attains—retains
Just the perfection; and there 's scarlet-skein
My ancient enemy, her lip and lip,
Sense-free, sense-frighting lips clenched cold and bold
Because of chin, that based resolve beneath!
Then the columnar neck completes the whole
Greek-sculpture-baffling body! Do I see?
Can I observe? You wait next word to come?
Well, wait and want! since no one blight I bid
Consume one least perfection. Each and all,
As they are rightly shocking now to me,
So may they still continue! Value them?
Ay, as the vendor knows the money-worth
O£ his Greek statue, fools aspire to buy,
And he to see the back of! Let as laugh!
You have absolved me from my sin at least!
You stand stout, strong, in the rude health of hate,
No touch of the tame timid nullity
My cowardice, forsooth, has practised on!
Ay, while you seemed to hint some fine fifth act
Of tragedy should freeze blood, end the farce,
I never doubted all was joke. I kept,
Maybe, an eye alert on paragraphs,
Newspaper-notice,—let no inquest slip,
Accident, disappearance: sound and safe
Were you, my victim, not of mind to die!
So, my worst fancy that could spoil the smooth
Of pillow, and arrest descent of sleep,
Was 'Into what dim hole can she have dived,
She and her wrongs, her woe that 's wearing flesh
And blood away?' Whereas, see, sorrow swells!
Or, fattened, fulsome, have you fed on me,
Sucked out my substance? How much gloss, I pray,
O'erbloomed those hair-swathes when there crept from you
To me that craze, else unaccountable,
Which urged me to contest our county-seat
With whom but my own brother's nominee?
Did that mouth's pulp glow ruby from carmine
While I misused my moment, pushed,—one word,—
One hair's-breadth more of gesture,—idiot-like
Past passion, floundered on to the grotesque,
And lost the heiress in a grin? At least,
You made no such mistake! You tickled fish,
Landed your prize the true artistic way!

How did the smug young curate rise to tune
Of 'Friend, a fatal fact divides us. Love
Suits me no longer. I have suffered shame,
Betrayal: past is past; the future—yours—
Shall never be contaminate by mine!
I might have spared me this confession, not
—Oh, never by some hideousest of lies,
Easy, impenetrable! No! but say,
By just the quiet answer—"I am cold."
Falsehood avaunt, each shadow of thee, hence!
Had happier fortune willed ... but dreams are vain.
Now, leave me—yes, for pity's sake!' Aha,
Who fails to see the curate as his face
Reddened and whitened, wanted handkerchief
At wrinkling brow and twinkling eye, until
Out burst the proper 'Angel, whom the fiend
Has thought to smirch,—thy whiteness, at one wipe
Of holy cambric, shall disgrace the swan!
Mine be the task' ... and so forth! Fool? not he!
Cunning in flavors, rather! What but sour
Suspected makes the sweetness doubly sweet,
And what stings love from faint to flamboyant
But the fear-sprinkle? Even horror helps—
Love's flame in me by such recited wrong
Drenched, quenched, indeed? It burns the fiercelier thence!'
Why, I have known men never love their wives
Till somebody—myself, suppose—had 'drenched
And quenched love,' so the blockheads whined: as if
The fluid fire that lifts the torpid limb
Were a wrong done to palsy. But I thrilled
No palsied person: half my age, or less,
The curate was, I 'll wager: o'er young blood
Your beauty triumphed! Eh, but—was it he?
Then, it was he, I heard of! None beside!
How frank you were about the audacious boy
Who fell upon you like a thunderbolt—
Passion and protestation! He it was
Reserved in petto! Ay, and 'rich' beside—
'Rich'—how supremely did disdain curl nose!
All that I heard was—'wedded to a priest;'
Informants sunk youth, riches and the rest.
And so my lawless love disparted loves,
That loves might come together with a rush!
Surely this last achievement sucked me dry:
Indeed, that way my wits went. Mistress-queen,
Be merciful and let your subject slink
Into dark safety! He 's a beggar, see—
Do not turn back his ship, Australia-bound,

And bid her land him right amid some crowd
Of creditors, assembled by your curse!
Don't cause the very rope to crack (you can!)
Whereon he spends his last (friend's) sixpence, just
The moment when he hoped to hang himself!
Be satisfied you beat him!"

She replies—

"Beat him! I do. To all that you confess
Of abject failure, I extend belief.
Your very face confirms it: God is just!
Let my face—fix your eyes!—in turn confirm
What I shall say. All-abject's but half truth;
Add to all-abject knave as perfect fool!
So is it you probed human nature, so
Prognosticated of me? Lay these words
To heart then, or where God meant heart should lurk!
That moment when you first revealed yourself,
My simple impulse prompted—end forthwith
The ruin of a life uprooted thus
To surely perish! How should such spoiled tree
Henceforward balk the wind of its worst sport,
Fail to go falling deeper, falling down
From sin to sin until some depth were reached
Doomed to the weakest by the wickedest
Of weak and wicked human-kind? But when,
That self-display made absolute,—behold
A new revealment!—round you pleased to veer,
Propose me what should prompt annul the past,
Make me 'amends by marriage'—in your phrase,
Incorporate me henceforth, body and soul,
With soul and body which mere brushing past
Brought leprosy upon me—'marry' these!
Why, then despair broke, reassurance dawned,
Clear-sighted was I that who hurled contempt
As I—thank God!—at the contemptible,
Was scarce an utter weakling. Rent away
By treason from my rightful pride of place,
I was not destined to the shame below.
A cleft had caught me: I might perish there,
But thence to be dislodged and whirled at last
Where the black torrent sweeps the sewage—no!
'Bare breast be on hard rock,' laughed out my soul
In gratitude, 'howe'er rock's grip may grind!
The plain, rough, wretched holdfast shall suffice
This wreck of me!' The wind,—I broke in bloom
At passage of,—which stripped me bole and branch,

Twisted me up and tossed me here,—turns back,
And, playful ever, would replant the spoil?
Be satisfied, not one least leaf that's mine
Shall henceforth help wind's sport to exercise!
Rather I give such remnant to the rock
Which never dreamed a straw would settle there.
Rock may not thank me, may not feel my breast,
Even: enough that I feel, hard and cold,
Its safety my salvation. Safe and saved,
I lived, live. When the tempter shall persuade
His prey to slip down, slide off, trust the wind,—
Now that I know if God or Satan be
Prince of the Power of the Air,—then, then, indeed,
Let my life end and degradation too!"

"Good!" he smiles, "true Lord Byron!" 'Tree and rock:
Rock,'—there's advancement! He's at first a youth,
Rich, worthless therefore; next he grows a priest:
Youth, riches prove a notable resource,
When to leave me for their possessor gluts
Malice abundantly; and now, last change,
The young rich parson represents a rock
—Bloodstone, no doubt. He's Evangelical?
Your Ritualists prefer the Church for spouse!"

She speaks.

"I have a story to relate.
There was a parish-priest, my father knew,
Elderly, poor: I used to pity him
Before I learned what woes are pity-worth.
Elderly was grown old now, scanty means
Were straitening fast to poverty, beside
The ailments which await in such a case.
Limited every way, a perfect man
Within the bounds built up and up since birth
Breast-high about him till the outside world
Was blank save o'erhead one blue bit of sky—
Faith: he had faith in dogma, small or great,
As in the fact that if he clave his skull
He'd find a brain there: who proves such a fact
No falsehood by experiment at price
Of soul and body? The one rule of life
Delivered him in childhood was 'Obey!
Labor!' He had obeyed and labored—tame,
True to the mill-track blinked on from above.
Some scholarship he may have gained in youth:
Gone—dropt or flung behind. Some blossom-flake,

Spring's boon, descends on every vernal head,
I used to think; but January joins
December, as his year had known no May;
Trouble its snow-deposit,—cold and old!
I heard it was his will to take a wife,
A helpmate. Duty bade him tend and teach—
How? with experience null, nor sympathy
Abundant,—while himself worked dogma dead,
Who would play ministrant to sickness, age,
Womankind, childhood? These demand a wife.
Supply the want, then! theirs the wife; for him—
No coarsest sample of the proper sex
But would have served his purpose equally
With God's own angel,—let but knowledge match
Her coarseness: zeal does only half the work.
I saw this—knew the purblind honest drudge
Was wearing out his simple blameless life,
And wanted help beneath a burden—borne
To treasure-house or dust-heap, what cared I?
Partner he needed: I proposed myself,
Nor much surprised him—duty was so clear!
Gratitude? What for? Gain of Paradise—
Escape, perhaps, from the dire penalty
Of who hides talent in a napkin? No:
His scruple was—should I be strong enough
—In body? since of weakness in the mind,
Weariness in the heart—no fear of these?
He took me as these Arctic voyagers
Take an aspirant to their toil and pain:
Can he endure them?—that 's the point, and not
—Will he? Who would not, rather! Whereupon,
I pleaded far more earnestly for leave
To give myself away, than you to gain
What you called priceless till you gained the heart
And soul and body! which, as beggars serve
Extorted alms, you straightway spat upon.
Not so my husband,—for I gained my suit,
And had my value put at once to proof.
Ask him! These four years I have died away
In village-life. The village? Ugliness
At best and filthiness at worst, inside.
Outside, sterility—earth sown with salt
Or what keeps even grass from growing fresh.
The life? I teach the poor and learn, myself,
That commonplace to such stupidity
Is all-recondite. Being brutalized
Their true need is brute-language, cheery grunts
And kindly cluckings, no articulate

Nonsense that 's elsewhere knowledge. Tend the sick,
Sickened myself at pig-perversity,
Cat-craft, dog-snarling—maybe, snapping" ...

"Brief:
You eat that root of bitterness called Man
—Raw: I prefer it cooked, with social sauce!
So, he was not the rich youth after all!
Well, I mistook. But somewhere needs must be
The compensation. If not young nor rich" ...

"You interrupt!"

"Because you 've daubed enough
Bistre for background. Play the artist now,
Produce your figure well-relieved in front!
The contrast—do not I anticipate?
Though neither rich nor young—what then? 'T is all
Forgotten, all this ignobility,
In the dear home, the darling word, the smile,
The something sweeter" ...

"Yes, you interrupt.
I have my purpose and proceed. Who lives
With beasts assumes beast-nature, look and voice,
And, much more, thought, for beasts think. Selfishness
In us met selfishness in them, deserved
Such answer as it gained. My husband, bent
On saving his own soul by saving theirs,—
They, bent on being saved if saving soul
Included body's getting bread and cheese
Somehow in life and somehow after death,—
Both parties were alike in the same boat,
One danger, therefore one equality.
Safety induces culture: culture seeks
To institute, extend and multiply
The difference between safe man and man,
Able to live alone now; progress means
What but abandonment of fellowship?
We were in common danger, still stuck close.
No new books,—were the old ones mastered yet?
No pictures and no music: these divert
—What from? the staving danger off! You paint
The waterspout above, you set to words
The roaring of the tempest round you? Thanks!
Amusement? Talk at end of the tired day
Of the more tiresome morrow! I transcribed
The page on page of sermon-scrawlings—stopped

Intellect's eye and ear to sense and sound—
Vainly: the sound and sense would penetrate
To brain and plague there in despite of me
Maddened to know more moral good were done
Had we two simply sallied forth and preached
I' the 'Green' they call their grimy,—I with twang
Of long-disused guitar,—with cut and slash
Of much-misvalued horsewhip he,—to bid
The peaceable come dance, the peace-breaker
Pay in his person! Whereas—Heaven and Hell,
Excite with that, restrain with this!—so dealt
His drugs my husband; as he dosed himself,
He drenched his cattle: and, for all my part
Was just to dub the mortar, never fear
But drugs, hand pestled at, have poisoned nose!
Heaven he let pass, left wisely undescribed:
As applicable therefore to the sleep
I want, that knows no waking—as to what 's
Conceived of as the proper prize to tempt
Souls less world-weary: there, no fault to find!
But Hell he made explicit. After death,
Life: man created new, ingeniously
Perfect for a vindictive purpose now,
That man, first fashioned in beneficence,
Was proved a failure; intellect at length
Replacing old obtuseness, memory
Made mindful of delinquent's bygone deeds
Now that remorse was vain, which life-long lay
Dormant when lesson might be laid to heart;
New gift of observation up and down
And round man's self, new power to apprehend
Each necessary consequence of act
In man for well or ill—things obsolete—
Just granted to supplant the idiocy
Man's only guide while act was yet to choose,
With ill or well momentously its fruit;
A faculty of immense suffering
Conferred on mind and body,—mind, erewhile
Unvisited by one compunctious dream
During sin's drunken slumber, startled up,
Stung through and through by sin's significance
Now that the holy was abolished—just
As body which, alive, broke down beneath
Knowledge, lay helpless in the path to good,
Failed to accomplish aught legitimate,
Achieve aught worthy,—which grew old in youth,
And at its longest fell a cut-down flower,—
Dying, this too revived by miracle

To bear no end of burden now that back
Supported torture to no use at all,
And live imperishably potent—since
Life's potency was impotent to ward
One plague off which made earth a hell before.
This doctrine, which one healthy view of things,
One sane sight of the general ordinance—
Nature—and its particular object—man,—
Which one mere eye-cast at the character
Of Who made these and gave man sense to boot,
Had dissipated once and evermore,—
This doctrine I have dosed our flock withal.
Why? Because none believed it. They desire
Such Heaven and dread such Hell, whom every day
The alehouse tempts from one, a dog-fight bids
Defy the other? All the harm is done
Ourselves—done my good husband who in youth
Perhaps read Dickens, done myself who still
Could play both Bach and Brahms. Such life I lead—
Thanks to you, knave! You learn its quality—
Thanks to me, fool!"

He eyes her earnestly,
But she continues.

"—Life which, thanks once more
To you, arch-knave as exquisitest fool,
I acquiescingly—I gratefully
Take back again to heart! and hence this speech
Which yesterday had spared you. Four years long
Life—I began to find intolerable,
Only this moment. Ere your entry just,
The leap of heart which answered, spite of me,
A friend's first summons, first provocative,
Authoritative, nay, compulsive call
To quit, though for a single day, my house
Of bondage—made return seem horrible.
I heard again a human lucid laugh
All trust, no fear; again saw earth pursue
Its narrow busy way amid small cares,
Smaller contentments, much weeds, some few flowers,—
Never suspicious of a thunderbolt
Avenging presently each daisy's death.
I recognized the beech-tree, knew the thrush
Repeated his old music-phrase,—all right,
How wrong was I, then! But your entry broke
Illusion, bade me back to bounds at once.
I honestly submit my soul: which sprang

At love, and losing love lies signed and sealed
'Failure.' No love more? then, no beauty more
Which tends to breed love! Purify my powers,
Effortless till some other world procures
Some other chance of prize! or, if none be,—
Nor second world nor chance,—undesecrate
Die then this aftergrowth of heart, surmised
Where May's precipitation left June blank!
Better have failed in the high aim, as I,
Than vulgarly in the low aim succeed
As, God be thanked, I do not! Ugliness
Had I called beauty, falsehood—truth, and you—
My lover! No—this earth's unchanged for me,
By his enchantment whom God made the Prince
O' the Power o' the Air, into a Heaven: there is
Heaven, since there is Heaven's simulation—earth.
I sit possessed in patience; prison-roof
Shall break one day and Heaven beam overhead."

His smile is done with; he speaks bitterly.

"Take my congratulations, and permit
I wish myself had proved as teachable!
—Or, no! until you taught me, could I learn,
A lesson from experience ne'er till now
Conceded? Please you listen while I show
How thoroughly you estimate my worth
And yours—the immeasurably superior! I
Believed at least in one thing, first to last,—
Your love to me: I was the vile and you
The precious; I abused you, I betrayed,
But doubted—never! Why else go my way
Judas-like plodding to this Potters' Field
Where fate now finds me? What has dinned my ear
And dogged my step? The spectre with the shriek
'Such she was, such were you, whose punishment
Is just!' And such she was not, all the while!
She never owned a love to outrage, faith
To pay with falsehood! For, my heart knows this—
Love once and you love always. Why, it 's down
Here in the Album: every lover knows
Love may use hate but—turn to hate, itself—
Turn even to indifference—no, indeed!
Well, I have been spellbound, deluded like
The witless negro by the Obeah-man
Who bids him wither: so, his eye grows dim,
His arm slack, arrow misses aim and spear
Goes wandering wide,—and all the woe because

He proved untrue to Fetish, who, he finds,
Was just a feather-phantom! I wronged love,
Am ruined,—and there was no love to wrong!"

"No love? Ah, dead love! I invoke thy ghost
To show the murderer where thy heart poured life
At summons of the stroke he doubts was dealt
On pasteboard and pretence! Not love, my love?
I changed for you the very laws of life:
Made you the standard of all right, all fair.
No genius but you could have been, no sage,
No sufferer—which is grandest—for the truth!
My hero—where the heroic only hid
To burst from hiding, brighten earth one day!
Age and decline were man's maturity;
Face, form were nature's type: more grace, more strength,
What had they been but just superfluous gauds,
Lawless divergence? I have danced through day
On tiptoe at the music of a word,
Have wondered where was darkness gone as night
Burst out in stars at brilliance of a smile!
Lonely, I placed the chair to help me seat
Your fancied presence; in companionship,
I kept my finger constant to your glove
Glued to my breast; then—where was all the world?
I schemed—not dreamed—how I might die some death
Should save your finger aching! Who creates
Destroys, he only: I had laughed to scorn
Whatever angel tried to shake my faith
And make you seem unworthy: you yourself
Only could do that! With a touch 't was done.
'Give me all, trust me wholly!' At the word,
I did give, I did trust—and thereupon
The touch did follow. Ah, the quiet smile,
The masterfully-folded arm in arm,
As trick obtained its triumph one time more!
In turn, my soul too triumphs in defeat:
Treason like faith moves mountains: love is gone!"

He paces to and fro, stops, stands quite close
And calls her by her name. Then—

"God forgives:
Forgive you, delegate of God, brought near
As never priests could bring him to this soul
That prays you both—forgive me! I abase—
Know myself mad and monstrous utterly
In all I did that moment; but as God

Gives me this knowledge—heart to feel and tongue
To testify—so be you gracious too!
Judge no man by the solitary work
Of—well, they do say and I can believe—
The devil in him: his, the moment,—mine
The life—your life!"

He names her name again.

"You were just—merciful as just, you were
In giving me no respite: punishment
Followed offending. Sane and sound once more,
The patient thanks decision, promptitude,
Which flung him prone and fastened him from hurt,
Haply to others, surely to himself.
I wake and would not you had spared one pang.
All's well that ends well!"

Yet again her name.

"Had you no fault? Why must you change, forsooth,
Parts, why reverse positions, spoil the play?
Why did your nobleness look up to me,
Not down on the ignoble thing confessed?
Was it your part to stoop, or lift the low?
Wherefore did God exalt you? Who would teach
The brute man's tameness and intelligence
Must never drop the dominating eye:
Wink—and what wonder if the mad fit break,
Followed by stripes and fasting? Sound and sane,
My life, chastised now, couches at your foot.
Accept, redeem me! Do your eyes ask 'How?'
I stand here penniless, a beggar; talk
What idle trash I may, this final blow
Of fortune fells me. I disburse, indeed,
This boy his winnings? when each bubble-scheme
That danced athwart my brain, a minute since,
The worse the better,—of repairing straight
My misadventure by fresh enterprise,
Capture of other boys in foolishness
His fellows,—when these fancies fade away
At first sight of the lost so long, the found
So late, the lady of my life, before
Whose presence I, the lost, am also found
Incapable of one least touch of mean
Expedient, I who teemed with plot and wile—
That family of snakes your eye bids flee!
Listen! Our troublesomest dreams die off

In daylight: I awake, and dream is—where?
I rouse up from the past: one touch dispels
England and all here. I secured long since
A certain refuge, solitary home
To hide in, should the head strike work one day,
The hand forget its cunning, or perhaps
Society grow savage,—there to end
My life's remainder, which, say what fools will,
Is or should be the best of life,—its fruit,
All tends to, root and stem and leaf and flower.
Come with me, love, loved once, loved only, come,
Blend loves there! Let this parenthetic doubt
Of love, in me, have been the trial test
Appointed to all flesh at some one stage
Of soul's achievement,—when the strong man doubts
His strength, the good man whether goodness be,
The artist in the dark seeks, fails to find
Vocation, and the saint forswears his shrine.
What if the lover may elude, no more
Than these, probative dark, must search the sky
Vainly for love, his soul's star? But the orb
Breaks from eclipse: I breathe again: I love!
Tempted, I fell; but fallen—fallen lie
Here at your feet, see! Leave this poor pretence
Of union with a nature and its needs
Repugnant to your needs and nature! Nay,
False, beyond falsity you reprehend
In me, is such mock marriage with such mere
Man-mask as—whom you witless wrong, beside,
By that expenditure of heart and brain
He recks no more of than would yonder tree
If watered with your life-blood: rains and dews
Answer its ends sufficiently, while me
One drop saves—sends to flower and fruit at last
The laggard virtue in the soul which else
Cumbers the ground! Quicken me! Call me yours—
Yours and the world's—yours and the world's and God's!
Yes, for you can, you only! Think! Confirm
Your instinct! Say, a minute since, I seemed
The castaway you count me,—all the more
Apparent shall the angelic potency
Lift me from out perdition's deep of deeps
To light and life and love!—that's love for you—
Love that already dares match might with yours.
You loved one worthy,—in your estimate,—
When time was; you descried the unworthy taint,
And where was love then? No such test could e'er
Try my love: but you hate me and revile;

Hatred, revilement—had you these to bear,
Would you, as I do, nor revile, nor hate,
But simply love on, love the more, perchance?
Abide by your own proof! 'Your love was love:
Its ghost knows no forgetting!' Heart of mine,
Would that I dared remember! Too unwise
Were he who lost a treasure, did himself
Enlarge upon the sparkling catalogue
Of gems to her his queen who trusted late
The keeper of her caskets! Can it be
That I, custodian of such relic still
As your contempt permits me to retain,
All I dare hug to breast is—'How your glove
Burst and displayed the long thin lily streak!'
What may have followed—that is forfeit now!
I hope the proud man has grown humble! True—
One grace of humbleness absents itself—
Silence! yet love lies deeper than all words,
And not the spoken but the speechless love
Waits answer ere I rise and go my way."

Whereupon, yet one other time the name.

To end she looks the large deliberate look,
Even prolongs it somewhat; then the soul
Bursts forth in a clear laugh that lengthens on,
On, till—thinned, softened, silvered, one might say
The bitter runnel hides itself in sand,
Moistens the hard gray grimly comic speech.

"Ay—give the baffled angler even yet
His supreme triumph as he hales to shore
A second time the fish once 'scaped from hook—
So artfully has new bait hidden old
Blood-imbrued iron! Ay, no barb's beneath
The gilded minnow here! You bid break trust,
This time, with who trusts me,—not simply bid
Me trust you, me who ruined but myself,
In trusting but myself! Since, thanks to you,
I know the feel of sin and shame,—be sure,
I shall obey you and impose them both
On one who happens to be ignorant
Although my husband—for the lure is love,
Your love! Try other tackle, fisher-friend!
Repentance, expiation, hopes and fears,
What you had been, may yet be, would I but
Prove helpmate to my hero—one and all
These silks and worsteds round the hook seduce

Hardly the late torn throat and mangled tongue.
Pack up, I pray, the whole assortment prompt!
Who wonders at variety of wile
In the Arch-cheat? You are the Adversary!
Your fate is of your choosing: have your choice!
Wander the world,—God has some end to serve,
Ere he suppress you! He waits: I endure,
But interpose no finger-tip, forsooth,
To stop your passage to the pit. Enough
That I am stable, uninvolved by you
In the rush downwards: free I gaze and fixed;
Your smiles, your tears, prayers, curses move alike
My crowned contempt. You kneel? Prostrate yourself!
To earth, and would the whole world saw you there!"

Whereupon—"All right!" carelessly begins
Somebody from outside, who mounts the stair,
And sends his voice for herald of approach:
Half in half out the doorway as the door
Gives way to push.

"Old fellow, all's no good!
The train's your portion! Lay the blame on me!
I'm no diplomatist, and Bismarck's self
Had hardly braved the awful Aunt at broach
Of proposition—so has world-repute
Preceded the illustrious stranger! Ah!"—

Quick the voice changes to astonishment,
Then horror, as the youth stops, sees, and knows.

The man who knelt starts up from kneeling, stands
Moving no muscle, and confronts the stare.

One great red outbreak buries—throat and brow—
The lady's proud pale queenliness of scorn:
Then her great eyes that turned so quick, become
Intenser:—quail at gaze, not they indeed!

V

It is the young man shatters silence first.

"Well, my lord—for indeed my lord you are,
I little guessed how rightly—this last proof
Of lordship-paramount confounds too much
My simple headpiece! Let's see how we stand

Each to the other! how we stood i' the game
Of life an hour ago,—the magpies, stile,
And oak-tree witnessed. Truth exchanged for truth—
My lord confessed his four-years-old affair—
How he seduced and then forsook the girl
Who married somebody and left him sad.
My pitiful experience was—I loved
A girl whose gown's hem had I dared to touch
My finger would have failed me, palsy-fixed.
She left me, sad enough, to marry—whom?
A better man,—then possibly not you!
How does the game stand? Who is who and what
Is what, o' the board now, since an hour went by?
My lord 's 'seduced, forsaken, sacrificed,'
Starts up, my lord's familiar instrument,
Associate and accomplice, mistress-slave—
Shares his adventure, follows on the sly!
—Ay, and since 'bag and baggage' is a phrase—
Baggage lay hid in carpet-bag belike,
Was but unpadlocked when occasion came
For holding council, since my back was turned,
On how invent ten thousand pounds which, paid,
Would lure the winner to lose twenty more,
Beside refunding these! Why else allow
The fool to gain them? So displays herself
The lady whom my heart believed—oh, laugh!
Noble and pure: whom my heart loved at once,
And who at once did speak truth when she said
'I am not mine now but another's'—thus
Being that other's! Devil's-marriage, eh?
'My lie weds thine till lucre us do part?'
But pity me the snobbish simpleton,
You two aristocratic tiptop swells
At swindling! Quits, I cry! Decamp content
With skin I 'm peeled of: do not strip bones bare—
As that you could, I have no doubt at all!
O you two rare ones! Male and female, Sir!
The male there smirked, this morning, 'Come, my boy—
Out with it! You've been crossed in love, I think:
I recognize the lover's hangdog look;
Make a clean breast and match my confidence,
For, I'll be frank, I too have had my fling,
Am punished for my fault, and smart enough!
Where now the victim hides her head, God knows!'
Here loomed her head, life-large, the devil knew!
Look out, Salvini! Here 's your man, your match!
He and I sat applauding, stall by stall,
Last Monday—'Here 's Othello' was our word,

'But where 's Iago?' Where? Why, there! And now
The fellow-artist, female specimen—
Oh, lady, you must needs describe yourself!
He 's great in art, but you—how greater still
—(If I can rightly, out of all I learned,
Apply one bit of Latin that assures
'Art means just art's concealment')—tower yourself!
For he stands plainly visible henceforth—
Liar and scamp: while you, in artistry
Prove so consummate—or I prove perhaps
So absolute an ass—that—either way—
You still do seem to me who worshipped you
And see you take the homage of this man,
Your master, who played slave and knelt, no doubt,
Before a mistress in his very craft ...
Well, take the fact, I nor believe my eyes,
Nor trust my understanding! Still you seem
Noble and pure as when we had the talk
Under the tower, beneath the trees, that day.
And there 's the key explains the secret: down
He knelt to ask your leave to rise a grade
I' the mystery of humbug: well he may!
For how you beat him! Half an hour ago,
I held your master for my best of friends;
And now I hate him! Four years since, you seemed
My heart's one love: well, and you so remain!
What 's he to you in craft?"

She looks him through.

"My friend, 't is just that friendship have its turn—
Interrogate thus me whom one, of foes
The worst, has questioned and is answered by.
Take you as frank an answer! answers both
Begin alike so far, divergent soon
World-wide—I own superiority
Over you, over him. As him I searched,
So do you stand seen through and through by me
Who, this time, proud, report your crystal shrines
A dewdrop, plain as amber prisons round
A spider in the hollow heart his house!
Nowise are you that thing my fancy feared
When out you stepped on me, a minute since,
—This man's confederate! no, you step not thus
Obsequiously at beck and call to help
At need some second scheme, and supplement
Guile by force, use my shame to pinion me
From struggle and escape! I fancied that!

Forgive me! Only by strange chance,—most strange
In even this strange world,—you enter now,
Obtain your knowledge. Me you have not wronged
Who never wronged you—least of all, my friend,
That day beneath the College tower and trees,
When I refused to say,—'not friend, but love!'
Had I been found as free as air when first
We met, I scarcely could have loved you. No—
For where was that in you which claimed return
Of love? My eyes were all too weak to probe
This other's seeming, but that seeming loved
The soul in me, and lied—I know too late!
While your truth was truth: and I knew at once
My power was just my beauty—bear the word—
As I must bear, of all my qualities,
To name the poorest one that serves my soul
And simulates myself! So much in me
You loved, I know: the something that 's beneath
Heard not your call,—uncalled, no answer comes!
For, since in every love, or soon or late,
Soul must awake and seek out soul for soul,
Yours, overlooking mine then, would, some day,
Take flight to find some other; so it proved—
Missing me, you were ready for this man.
I apprehend the whole relation: his—
The soul wherein you saw your type of worth
At once, true object of your tribute. Well
Might I refuse such half-heart's homage! Love
Divining, had assured you I no more
Stand his participant in infamy
Than you—I need no love to recognize
As simply dupe and nowise fellow-cheat!
Therefore accept one last friend's-word,—your friend's,
All men's friend, save a felon's. Ravel out
The bad embroilment howsoe'er you may,
Distribute as it please you praise or blame
To me—so you but fling this mockery far—
Renounce this rag-and-feather hero-sham,
This poodle clipt to pattern, lion-like!
Throw him his thousands back, and lay to heart
The lesson I was sent,—if man discerned
Ever God's message,—just to teach. I judge—
To far another issue than could dream
Your cousin,—younger, fairer, as befits—
Who summoned me to judgment's exercise.
I find you, save in folly, innocent.
And in my verdict lies your fate; at choice
Of mine your cousin takes or leaves you. 'Take!'

I bid her—for you tremble back to truth!
She turns the scale,—one touch of the pure hand
Shall so press down, emprison past relapse
Farther vibration 'twixt veracity—
That 's honest solid earth—and falsehood, theft
And air, that 's one illusive emptiness!
That reptile capture you? I conquered him:
You saw him cower before me! Have no fear
He shall offend you farther. Spare to spurn—
Safe let him slink hence till some subtler Eve
Than I, anticipate the snake—bruise head
Ere he bruise heel—or, warier than the first,
Some Adam purge earth's garden of its pest
Before the slaver spoil the Tree of Life!

"You! Leave this youth, as he leaves you, as I
Leave each! There 's caution surely extant yet
Though conscience in you were too vain a claim.
Hence quickly! Keep the cash but leave unsoiled
The heart I rescue and would lay to heal
Beside another's! Never let her know
How near came taint of your companionship!"

"Ah"—draws a long breath with a new strange look
The man she interpellates—soul astir
Under its covert, as, beneath the dust,
A coppery sparkle all at once denotes
The hid snake has conceived a purpose.

"Ah—
Innocence should be crowned with ignorance?
Desirable indeed, but difficult!
As if yourself, now, had not glorified
Your helpmate by imparting him a hint
Of how a monster made the victim bleed
Ere crook and courage saved her—hint, I say,—
Not the whole horror,—that were needless risk,—
But just such inkling, fancy of the fact,
As should suffice to qualify henceforth
The shepherd, when another lamb would stray,
For warning "Ware the wolf!' No doubt at all,
Silence is generosity,—keeps wolf
Unhunted by flock's warder! Excellent,
Did—generous to me, mean—just to him!
But, screening the deceiver, lamb were found
Outraging the deceitless! So,—he knows!
And yet, unharmed I breathe—perchance, repent—
Thanks to the mercifully-politic!"

"Ignorance is not innocence but sin—
Witness yourself ignore what after-pangs
Pursue the plague-infected. Merciful
Am I? Perhaps! the more contempt, the less
Hatred; and who so worthy of contempt
As you that rest assured I cooled the spot
I could not cure, by poisoning, forsooth,
Whose hand I pressed there? Understand for once
That, sick, of all the pains corroding me
This burnt the last and nowise least—the need
Of simulating soundness. I resolved—
No matter how the struggle tasked weak flesh—
To hide the truth away as in a grave
From—most of all—my husband: he nor knows
Nor ever shall be made to know your part,
My part, the devil's part,—I trust, God's part
In the foul matter. Saved, I yearn to save
And not destroy: and what destruction like
The abolishing of faith in him, that's faith
In me as pure and true? Acquaint some child
Who takes yon tree into his confidence,
That, where he sleeps now, was a murder done,
And that the grass which grows so thick, he thinks,
Only to pillow him is product just
Of what lies festering beneath! 'T is God
Must bear such secrets and disclose them. Man?
The miserable thing I have become
By dread acquaintance with my secret—you—
That thing had he become by learning me—
The miserable, whom his ignorance
Would wrongly call the wicked: ignorance
Being, I hold, sin ever, small or great.
No, he knows nothing!"

"He and I alike
Are bound to you for such discreetness, then.
What if our talk should terminate awhile?
Here is a gentleman to satisfy,
Settle accounts with, pay ten thousand pounds
Before we part—as, by his face, I fear,
Results from your appearance on the scene.
Grant me a minute's parley with my friend
Which scarce admits of a third personage!
The room from which you made your entry first
So opportunely—still untenanted—
What if you please return there? Just a word
To my young friend first—then, a word to you,

And you depart to fan away each fly
From who, grass-pillowed, sleeps so sound at home!"

"So the old truth comes back! A wholesome change,—
At last the altered eye, the rightful tone!
But even to the truth that drops disguise
And stands forth grinning malice which but now
Whined so contritely—I refuse assent
Just as to malice. I, once gone, come back?
No, my lord! I enjoy the privilege
Of being absolutely loosed from you
Too much—the knowledge that your power is null
Which was omnipotence. A word of mouth,
A wink of eye would have detained me once,
Body and soul your slave; and now, thank God,
Your fawningest of prayers, your frightfulest
Of curses—neither would avail to turn
My footstep for a moment!"

"Prayer, then, tries
No such adventure. Let us cast about
For something novel in expedient: take
Command,—what say you? I profess myself
One fertile in resource. Commanding, then,
I bid—not only wait there, but return
Here, where I want you! Disobey and—good!
On your own head the peril!"

"Come!" breaks in
The boy with his good glowing face. "Shut up!
None of this sort of thing while I stand here
—Not to stand that! No bullying, I beg!
I also am to leave you presently
And never more set eyes upon your face—
You won't mind that much; but—I tell you frank—
I do mind having to remember this
For your last word and deed—my friend who were!
Bully a woman you have ruined, eh?
Do you know,—I give credit all at once
To all those stories everybody told
And nobody but I would disbelieve:
They all seem likely now,—nay, certain, sure!
I daresay you did cheat at cards that night
The row was at the Club: 'sauter la coupe'—
That was your 'cut,' for which your friends 'cut' you;
While I, the booby, 'cut'—acquaintanceship
With who so much as laughed when I said 'luck!'
I daresay you had bets against the horse

They doctored at the Derby; little doubt,
That fellow with the sister found you shirk
His challenge and did kick you like a ball,
Just as the story went about! Enough:
It only serves to show how well advised,
Madam, you were in bidding such a fool
As I, go hang. You see how the mere sight
And sound of you suffice to tumble down
Conviction topsy-turvy: no,—that 's false,—
There 's no unknowing what one knows; and yet
Such is my folly that, in gratitude
For ... well, I 'm stupid; but you seemed to wish
I should know gently what I know, should slip
Softly from old to new, not break my neck
Between beliefs of what you were and are.
Well then, for just the sake of such a wish
To cut no worse a figure than needs must
In even eyes like mine, I 'd sacrifice
Body and soul! But don't think danger—pray!—
Menaces either! He do harm to us?
Let me say 'us' this one time! You 'd allow
I lent perhaps my hand to rid your ear
Of some cur's yelping—hand that 's fortified,
Into the bargain, with a horsewhip? Oh,
One crack and you shall see how curs decamp!—
My lord, you know your losses and my gains.
Pay me my money at the proper time!
If cash be not forthcoming—well, yourself
Have taught me, and tried often, I 'll engage,
The proper course: I post you at the Club,
Pillory the defaulter. Crack, to-day,
Shall, slash, to-morrow, slice through flesh and bone!
There, Madam, you need mind no cur, I think!"

"Ah, what a gain to have an apt no less
Thou grateful scholar! Nay, he brings to mind
My knowledge till he puts me to the blush,
So long has it lain rusty! Post my name!
That were indeed a wheal from whipcord! Whew!
I wonder now if I could rummage out
—Just to match weapons—some old scorpion-scourge!
Madam, you hear my pupil, may applaud
His triumph o'er the master. I—no more
Bully, since I 'm forbidden: but entreat—
Wait and return—for my sake, no! but just
To save your own defender, should he chance
Get thwacked through awkward flourish of his thong.
And what if—since all waiting 's weary work—

I help the time pass 'twixt your exit now
And entry then? for—pastime proper—here 's
The very thing, the Album, verse and prose
To make the laughing minutes launch away!
Each of us must contribute. I 'll begin—
'Hail, calm acclivity, salubrious spot!'
I 'm confident I beat the bard,—for why?
My young friend owns me an Iago—him
Confessed, among the other qualities,
A ready rhymer. Oh, he rhymed! Here goes!
—Something to end with 'horsewhip!' No, that rhyme
Beats me; there 's 'cowslip,' 'boltsprit,' nothing else!
So, Tennyson take my benison,—verse for bard,
Prose suits the gambler's book best! Dared and done!"

Wherewith he dips pen, writes a line or two,
Closes and clasps the cover, gives the book,
Bowing the while, to her who hesitates,
Turns half away, turns round again, at last
Takes it as you touch carrion, then retires.
The door shuts fast the couple.

VI

With a change
Of his whole manner, opens out at once
The Adversary.

"Now, my friend, for you!
You who, protected late, aggressive grown,
Brandish, it seems, a weapon I must 'ware!
Plain speech in me becomes respectable
Henceforth because courageous; plainly, then—
(Have lash well loose, hold handle tight and light!)
Throughout my life's experience, you indulged
Yourself and friend by passing in review
So courteously but now, I vainly search
To find one record of a specimen
So perfect of the pure and simple fool
As this you furnish me. Ingratitude
I lump with folly,—all 's one lot,—so—fool!
Did I seek you or you seek me? Seek? sneak
For service to, and service you would style—
And did style—godlike, scarce an hour ago!
Fool, there again, yet not precisely there
First-rate in folly: since the hand you kissed
Did pick you from the kennel, did plant firm

Your footstep on the pathway, did persuade
Your awkward shamble to true gait and pace,
Fit for the world you walk in. Once a-strut
On that firm pavement which your cowardice
Was for renouncing as a pitfall, next
Came need to clear your brains of their conceit
They cleverly could distinguish who was who,
Whatever folk might tramp the thoroughfare.
Men, now—familiarly you read them off,
Each phiz at first sight! Oh, you had an eye!
Who couched it? made you disappoint each fox
Eager to strip my gosling of his fluff
So golden as he cackled 'Goose trusts lamb'?
'Ay, but I saved you—wolf defeated fox—
Wanting to pick your bones myself?' then, wolf
Has got the worst of it with goose for once.
I, penniless, pay you ten thousand pounds
(—No gesture, pray! I pay ere I depart!)
And how you turn advantage to account
Here 's the example! Have I proved so wrong
In my peremptory 'debt must be discharged'?
Oh, you laughed lovelily, were loth to leave
The old friend out at elbows, pooh, a thing
Not to be thought of! I must keep my cash,
And you forget your generosity!
Ha ha! I took your measure when I laughed
My laugh to that! First quarrel—nay, first faint
Pretence at taking umbrage—'Down with debt,
Both interest and principal!—The Club,
Exposure and expulsion!—stamp me out!'
That 's the magnanimous magnificent
Renunciation of advantage! Well,
But whence and why did you take umbrage, Sir?
Because your master, having made you know
Somewhat of men, was minded to advance,
Expound you women, still a mystery!
My pupil pottered with a cloud, on brow,
A clod in breast: had loved, and vainly loved:
Whence blight and blackness, just for all the world
As Byron used to teach us boys. Thought I—
'Quick rid him of that rubbish! Clear the cloud,
And set the heart a-pulsing!'—heart, this time:
'T was nothing but the head I doctored late
For ignorance of Man; now heart 's to dose,
Palsied by over-palpitation due
To Woman-worship—so, to work at once
On first avowal of the patient's ache!
This morning you described your malady,—

How you dared love a piece of virtue—lost
To reason, as the upshot showed: for scorn
Fitly repaid your stupid arrogance;
And, parting, you went two ways, she resumed
Her path—perfection, while forlorn you paced
The world that 's made for beasts like you and me.
My remedy was—tell the fool the truth!
Your paragon of purity had plumped
Into these arms at their first outspread—'fallen
My victim,' she prefers to turn the phrase—
And, in exchange for that frank confidence,
Asked for my whole life present and to come—
Marriage: a thing uncovenanted for!
Never so much as put in question! Life—
Implied by marriage—throw that trifle in
And round the bargain off, no otherwise
Than if, when we played cards, because you won
My money you should also want my head!
That, I demurred to: we but played 'for love'—
She won my love; had she proposed for stakes,
'Marriage,'—why, that 's for whist, a wiser game.
Whereat she raved at me, as losers will,
And went her way. So far the story 's known,
The remedy 's applied, no farther—which
Here 's the sick man's first honorarium for—
Posting his medicine-monger at the Club!
That being, Sir, the whole you mean my fee—
In gratitude for such munificence
I 'm bound in common honesty to spare
No droplet of the draught: so,—pinch your nose,
Pull no wry faces!—drain it to the dregs!
I say 'She went off'—'went off,' you subjoin,
'Since not to wedded bliss, as I supposed,
Sure to some convent: solitude and peace
Help her to hide the shame from mortal view,
With prayer and fasting.' No, my sapient Sir!
Far wiselier, straightway she betook herself
To a prize-portent from the donkey-show
Of leathern long-ears that compete for palm
In clerical absurdity: since he,
Good ass, nor practises the shaving-trick,
The candle-crotchet, nonsense which repays
When you 've young ladies congregant,—but schools
The poor,—toils, moils, and grinds the mill, nor means
To stop and munch one thistle in this life
Till next life smother him with roses: just
The parson for her purpose! Him she stroked
Over the muzzle; into mouth with bit,

And on to back with saddle,—there he stood,
The serviceable beast who heard, believed
And meekly bowed him to the burden,—borne
Off in a canter to seclusion—ay,
The lady 's lost! But had a friend of mine
—While friend he was—imparted his sad case
To sympathizing counsellor, full soon
One cloud at least had vanished from his brow.
'Don't fear!' had followed reassuringly—
The lost will in due time turn up again,
Probably just when, weary of the world,
You think of nothing less than settling-down
To country life and golden days, beside
A dearest best and brightest virtuousest
Wife: who needs no more hope to hold her own
Against the naughty-and-repentant—no,
Than water-gruel against Roman punch!'
And as I prophesied, it proves! My youth,—
Just at the happy moment when, subdued
To spooniness, he finds that youth fleets fast,
That town-life tires, that men should drop boys'-play,
That property, position have, no doubt,
Their exigency with their privilege,
And if the wealthy wed with wealth, how dire
The double duty!—in, behold, there beams
Our long-lost lady, form and face complete!
And where 's my moralizing pupil now,
Had not his master missed a train by chance?
But, by your side instead of whirled away,
How have I spoiled scene, stopped catastrophe,
Struck flat the stage-effect I know by heart!
Sudden and strange the meeting—improvised?
Bless you, the last event she hoped or dreamed!
But rude sharp stroke will crush out fire from flint—
Assuredly from flesh. ''T is you?' 'Myself!'
'Changed?' 'Changeless!' 'Then, what's earth to me?' 'To me
What 's heaven?' 'So,—thine!' 'And thine!'
'And likewise mine!'
Had laughed 'Amen' the devil, but for me
Whose intermeddling hinders this hot haste,
And bids you, ere concluding contract, pause—
Ponder one lesson more, then sign and seal
At leisure and at pleasure,—lesson's price
Being, if you have skill to estimate,
—How say you?—I 'm discharged my debt in full!
Since paid you stand, to farthing uttermost,
Unless I fare like that black majesty
A friend of mine had visit from last Spring.

Coasting along the Cape-side, he 's becalmed
Off an uncharted bay, a novel town
Untouched at by the trader: here 's a chance!
Out paddles straight the king in his canoe,
Comes over bulwark, says he means to buy
Ship's cargo—being rich and having brought
A treasure ample for the purpose. See!
Four dragons, stalwart blackies, guard the same
Wrapped round and round: its hulls, a multitude,—
Palm-leaf and cocoa-mat and goat's-hair cloth
All duly braced about with bark and board,—
Suggest how brave, 'neath coat, must kernel be!
At length the peeling is accomplished, plain
The casket opens out its core, and lo
—A brand-new British silver sixpence—bid
That 's ample for the Bank,—thinks majesty!
You are the Captain; call my sixpence cracked
Or copper; 'what I 've said is calumny;
The lady 's spotless!' Then,—I 'll prove my words,
Or make you prove them true as truth—yourself,
Here, on the instant! I 'll not mince my speech,
Things at this issue. When she enters, then,
Make love to her! No talk of marriage now—
The point-blank bare proposal! Pick no phrase—
Prevent all misconception! Soon you 'll see
How different the tactics when she deals
With an instructed man, no longer boy
Who blushes like a booby. Woman's wit!
Man, since you have instruction, blush no more!
Such your five minutes' profit by my pains,
'T is simply now,—demand and be possessed!
Which means—you may possess—may strip the tree
Of fruit desirable to make one wise!
More I nor wish nor want: your act 's your act,
My teaching is but—there 's the fruit to pluck
Or let alone at pleasure. Next advance
In knowledge were beyond you! Don't expect
I bid a novice—pluck, suck, send sky-high
Such fruit, once taught that neither crab nor sloe
Falls readier prey to who but robs a hedge,
Than this gold apple to my Hercules.
Were you no novice but proficient—then,
Then, truly, I might prompt you—Touch and taste,
Try flavor and be tired as soon as I!
Toss on the prize to greedy mouths agape,
Betake yours, sobered as the satiate grow,
To wise man's solid meal of house and land,
Consols and cousin! but, my boy, my boy,

Such lore 's above you!

Here 's the lady back!
So, Madam, you have conned the Album-page
And come to thank its last contributor?
How kind and condescending! I retire
A moment, lest I spoil the interview,
And mar my own endeavor to make friends—
You with him, him with you, and both with me!
If I succeed—permit me to inquire
Five minutes hence! Friends bid good-by, you know."—
And out he goes.

VII

She, face, form, bearing, one
Superb composure—

"He has told you all?
Yes, he has told you all, your silence says—
What gives him, as he thinks, the mastery
Over my body and my soul!—has told
That instance, even, of their servitude
He now exacts of me? A silent blush!
That 's well, though better would white ignorance
Beseem your brow, undesecrate before—
Ay, when I left you! I too learn at last
—Hideously learned as I seemed so late—
What sin may swell to. Yes,—I needed learn
That, when my prophet's rod became the snake
I fled from, it would, one day, swallow up
—Incorporate whatever serpentine
Falsehood and treason and unmanliness
Beslime earth's pavement: such the power of Hell,
And so beginning, ends no otherwise
The Adversary! I was ignorant,
Blameworthy—if you will; but blame I take
Nowise upon me as I ask myself
—You—how can you, whose soul I seemed to read
The limpid eyes through, have declined so deep,
Even with him for consort? I revolve
Much memory, pry into the looks and words
Of that day's walk beneath the College wall,
And nowhere can distinguish, in what gleams
Only pure marble through my dusky past,
A dubious cranny where such poison-seed
Might harbor, nourish what should yield to-day

This dread ingredient for the cup I drink.
Do not I recognize and honor truth
In seeming?—take your truth, and for return,
Give you my truth, a no less precious gift?
You loved me: I believed you. I replied
—How could I other?—'I was not my own,'
No longer had the eyes to see, the ears
To hear, the mind to judge, since heart and soul
Now were another's. My own right in me,
For well or ill, consigned away—my face
Fronted the honest path, deflection whence
Had shamed me in the furtive backward look
At the late bargain—fit such chapman's phrase!—
As though—less hasty and more provident—
Waiting had brought advantage. Not for me
The chapman's chance! Yet while thus much was true,
I spared you—as I knew you then—one more
Concluding word which, truth no less, seemed best
Buried away forever. Take it now,
Its power to pain is past! Four years—that day—
Those limes that make the College avenue!
I would that—friend and foe—by miracle,
I had, that moment, seen into the heart
Of either, as I now am taught to see!
I do believe I should have straight assumed
My proper function, and sustained a soul,
—Nor aimed at being just sustained myself
By some man's soul—the weaker woman's-want!
So had I missed the momentary thrill
Of finding me in presence of a god,
But gained the god's own feeling when he gives
Such thrill to what turns life from death before.
'Gods many and Lords many,' says the Book:
You would have yielded up your soul to me
—Not to the false god who has burned its clay
In his own image. I had shed my love
Like Spring dew on the clod all flowery thence,
Not sent up a wild vapor to the sun
That drinks and then disperses. Both of us
Blameworthy,—I first meet my punishment—
And not so hard to bear. I breathe again!
Forth from those arms' enwinding leprosy
At last I struggle—uncontaminate:
Why must I leave you pressing to the breast
That 's all one plague-spot? Did you love me once?
Then take love's last and best return! I think,
Womanliness means only motherhood;
All love begins and ends there,—roams enough,

But, having run the circle, rests at home.
Why is your expiation yet to make?
Pull shame with your own hands from your own head
Now,—never wait the slow envelopment
Submitted to by unelastic age!
One fierce throe frees the sapling: flake on flake
Lull till they leave the oak snow-stupefied.
Your heart retains its vital warmth—or why
That blushing reassurance? Blush, young blood!
Break from beneath this icy premature
Captivity of wickedness—I warn
Back, in God's name! No fresh encroachment here!
This May breaks all to bud—no winter now!
Friend, we are both forgiven! Sin no more!
I am past sin now, so shall you become!
Meanwhile I testify that, lying once,
My foe lied ever, most lied last of all.
He, waking, whispered to your sense asleep
The wicked counsel,—and assent might seem;
But, roused, your healthy indignation breaks
The idle dream-pact. You would die—not dare
Confirm your dream-resolve,—nay, find the word
That fits the deed to bear the light of day!
Say I have justly judged you! then farewell
To blushing—nay, it ends in smiles, not tears!
Why tears now? I have justly judged, thank God!"

He does blush boy-like, but the man speaks out,
—Makes the due effort to surmount himself.

"I don't know what he wrote—how should I? Nor
How he could read my purpose, which, it seems,
He chose to somehow write—mistakenly
Or else for mischief's sake. I scarce believe
My purpose put before you fair and plain
Would need annoy so much; but there's my luck—
From first to last I blunder. Still, one more
Turn at the target, try to speak my thought!
Since he could guess my purpose, won't you read
Right what he set down wrong? He said—let 's think!
Ay, so!—he did begin by telling heaps
Of tales about you. Now, you see—suppose
Any one told me—my own mother died
Before I knew her—told me—to his cost!—
Such tales about my own dead mother: why,
You would not wonder surely if I knew,
By nothing but my own heart's help, he lied,
Would you? No reason 's wanted in the case.

So with you! In they burnt on me, his tales,
Much as when madhouse-inmates crowd around,
Make captive any visitor and scream
All sorts of stories of their keeper—he 's
Both dwarf and giant, vulture, wolf, dog, cat,
Serpent and scorpion, yet man all the same;
Sane people soon see through the gibberish!
I just made out, you somehow lived somewhere
A life of shame—I can't distinguish more—
Married or single—how, don't matter much:
Shame which himself had caused—that point was clear,
That fact confessed—that thing to hold and keep.
Oh, and he added some absurdity
—That you were here to make me—ha, ha, ha!—
Still love you, still of mind to die for you,
Ha, ha—as if that needed mighty pains!
Now, foolish as ... but never mind myself;
—What I am, what I am not, in the eye
Of the world, is what I never cared for much.
Fool then or no fool, not one single word
In the whole string of lies did I believe,
But this—this only—if I choke, who cares?—
I believe somehow in your purity
Perfect as ever! Else what use is God?
He is God, and work miracles he can!
Then, what shall I do? Quite as clear, my course!
They 've got a thing they call their Labyrinth
I' the garden yonder: and my cousin played
A pretty trick once, led and lost me deep
Inside the briery maze of hedge round hedge;
And there might I be staying now, stock-still,
But that I laughing bade eyes follow nose
And so straight pushed my path through let and stop
And soon was out in the open, face all scratched,
But well behind my back the prison-bars
In sorry plight enough, I promise you!
So here: I won my way to truth through lies—
Said, as I saw light,—if her shame be shame
I 'll rescue and redeem her,—shame 's no shame?
Then, I 'll avenge, protect—redeem myself
The stupidest of sinners! Here I stand!
Dear,—let me once dare call you so,—you said,
Thus ought you to have done, four years ago,
Such things and such! Ay, dear, and what ought I?
You were revealed to me: where 's gratitude,
Where 's memory even, where the gain of you
Discernible in my low after-life
Of fancied consolation? why, no horse

Once fed on corn, will, missing corn, go munch
Mere thistles like a donkey! I missed you,
And in your place found—him, made him my love,
Ay, did I,—by this token, that he taught
So much beast-nature that I meant ... God knows
Whether I bow me to the dust enough! ..
To marry—yes, my cousin here! I hope
That was a master-stroke! Take heart of hers,
And give her hand of mine with no more heart
Than now you see upon this brow I strike!
What atom of a heart do I retain
Not all yours? Dear, you know it! Easily
May she accord me pardon when I place
My brow beneath her foot, if foot so deign,
Since uttermost indignity is spared—
Mere marriage and no love! And all this time
Not one word to the purpose! Are you free?
Only wait! only let me serve—deserve
Where you appoint and how you see the good!
I have the will—perhaps the power—at least
Means that have power against the world. For time—
Take my whole life for your experiment!
If you are bound—in marriage, say—why, still,
Still, sure, there 's something for a friend to do,
Outside? A mere well-wisher, understand!
I 'll sit, my life long, at your gate, you know,
Swing it wide open to let you and him
Pass freely,—and you need not look, much less
Fling me a 'Thank you—are you there, old friend?'
Don't say that even: I should drop like shot!
So I feel now at least: some day, who knows?
After no end of weeks and months and years
You might smile 'I believe you did your best!'
And that shall make my heart leap—leap such leap
As lands the feet in Heaven to wait you there!
Ah, there 's just one thing more! How pale you look!
Why? Are you angry? If there 's, after all,
Worst come to worst—if still there somehow be
The shame—I said was no shame,—none, I swear!—
In that case, if my hand and what it holds,—
My name,—might be your safeguard now—at once—
Why, here 's the hand—you have the heart! Of course—
No cheat, no binding you, because I'm bound,
To let me off probation by one day,
Week, month, year, lifetime! Prove as you propose!
Here 's the hand with the name to take or leave!
That 's all—and no great piece of news, I hope!"

"Give me the hand, then!" she cries hastily.
"Quick, now! I hear his footstep!"

Hand in hand
The couple face him as he enters, stops
Short, stands surprised a moment, laughs away
Surprise, resumes the much-experienced man.

"So, you accept him?"

"Till us death do part!"

"No longer? Come, that 's right and rational!
I fancied there was power in common sense,
But did not know it worked thus promptly. Well—
At last each understands the other, then?
Each drops disguise, then? So, at supper-time
These masquerading people doff their gear,
Grand Turk his pompous turban, Quakeress
Her stiff-starched bib and tucker,—make-believe
That only bothers when, ball-business done,
Nature demands champagne and mayonnaise.
Just so has each of us sage three abjured
His and her moral pet particular
Pretension to superiority,
And, cheek by jowl, we henceforth munch and joke!
Go, happy pair, paternally dismissed
To live and die together—for a month,
Discretion can award no more! Depart
From whatsoe'er the calm sweet solitude
Selected—Paris not improbably—
At month's end, when the honeycomb 's left wax,
—You, daughter, with a pocketful of gold
Enough to find your village boys and girls
In duffel cloaks and hobnailed shoes from May
To—what 's the phrase?—Christmas-come-never-mas!
You, son and heir of mine, shall reappear
Ere Spring-time, that 's the ring-time, lose one leaf,
And—not without regretful smack of lip
The while you wipe it free of honey-smear—
Marry the cousin, play the magistrate,
Stand for the county, prove perfection's pink—
Master of hounds, gay-coated dine—nor die
Sooner than needs of gout, obesity,
And sons at Christ Church! As for me,—ah me,
I abdicate—retire on my success,
Four years well occupied in teaching youth
—My son and daughter the exemplary!

Time for me to retire now, having placed
Proud on their pedestal the pair: in turn,
Let them do homage to their master! You,—
Well, your flushed cheek and flashing eye proclaim
Sufficiently your gratitude: you paid
The honorarium, the ten thousand pounds
To purpose, did you not? I told you so!
And you,—but, bless me, why so pale—so faint
At influx of good fortune? Certainly,
No matter how or why or whose the fault,
I save your life—save it, nor less nor more!
You blindly were resolved to welcome death
In that black boor-and-bumpkin-haunted hole
Of his, the prig with all the preachments! You
Installed as nurse and matron to the crones
And wenches, while there lay a world outside
Like Paris (which again I recommend),
In company and guidance of—first, this,
Then—all in good time—some new friend as fit—
What if I were to say, some fresh myself,
As I once figured? Each dog has his day,
And mine 's at sunset: what should old dog do
But eye young litters' frisky puppyhood?
Oh, I shall watch this beauty and this youth
Frisk it in brilliance! But don't fear! Discreet,
I shall pretend to no more recognize
My quondam pupils than the doctor nods
When certain old acquaintances may cross
His path in Park, or sit down prim beside
His plate at dinner-table: tip nor wink
Scares patients he has put, for reason good,
Under restriction,—maybe, talked sometimes
Of douche or horsewhip to,—for why? because
The gentleman would crazily declare
His best friend was—Iago! Ay, and worse—
The lady, all at once grown lunatic,
In suicidal monomania vowed,
To save her soul, she needs must starve herself!
They 're cured now, both, and I tell nobody.
Why don't you speak? Nay, speechless, each of you
Can spare—without unclasping plighted troth—
At least one hand to shake! Left-hands will do—
Yours first, my daughter! Ah, it guards—it gripes
The precious Album fast—and prudently!
As well obliterate the record there
On page the last: allow me tear the leaf!
Pray, now! And afterward, to make amends,
What if all three of us contribute each

A line to that prelusive fragment,—help
The embarrassed bard who broke out to break down
Dumfoundered at such unforeseen success?
'Hail, calm acclivity, salubrious spot'
You begin—place aux dames! I 'll prompt you then!
'Here do I take the good the gods allot!'
Next you, Sir! What, still sulky? Sing, O Muse!
'Here does my lord in full discharge his shot!'
Now for the crowning flourish! mine shall be" ...

"Nothing to match your first effusion, mar
What was, is, shall remain your masterpiece!
Authorship has the alteration-itch!
No, I protest against erasure. Read,
My friend!" (she gasps out). "Read and quickly read
'Before us death do part,' what made you mine
And made me yours—the marriage-license here!
Decide if he is like to mend the same!"

And so the lady, white to ghastliness,
Manages somehow to display the page
With left-hand only, while the right retains
The other hand, the young man's,—dreaming-drunk
He, with this drench of stupefying stuff,
Eyes wide, mouth open,—half the idiot's stare
And half the prophet's insight,—holding tight,
All the same, by his one fact in the world—
The lady's right-hand: he but seems to read—
Does not, for certain; yet, how understand
Unless he reads?

So, understand he does,
For certain. Slowly, word by word, she reads
Aloud that license—or that warrant, say.

"One against two—and two that urge their odds
To uttermost—I needs must try resource!
Madam, I laid me prostrate, bade you spurn
Body and soul: you spurned and safely spurned
So you had spared me the superfluous taunt
'Prostration means no power to stand erect,
Stand, trampling on who trampled—prostrate now!'
So, with my other fool-foe: I was fain
Let the boy touch me with the buttoned foil.
And him the infection gains, he too must needs
Catch up the butcher's cleaver. Be it so!
Since play turns earnest, here 's my serious fence.
He loves you; he demands your love: both know

What love means in my language. Love him then!
Pursuant to a pact, love pays my debt:
Therefore, deliver me from him, thereby
Likewise delivering from me yourself!
For, hesitate—much more, refuse consent—
I tell the whole truth to your husband. Flat
Cards lie on table, in our gamester-phrase!
Consent—you stop my mouth, the only way."

"I did well, trusting instinct: knew your hand
Had never joined with his in fellowship
Over this pact of infamy. You known—
As he was known through every nerve of me.
Therefore I 'stopped his mouth the only way'
But my way! none was left for you, my friend—
The loyal—near, the loved one! No—no—no!
Threaten? Chastise? The coward would but quail.
Conquer who can, the cunning of the snake!
Stamp out his slimy strength from tail to head,
And still you leave vibration of the tongue.
His malice had redoubled—not on me
Who, myself, choose my own refining fire—
But on poor unsuspicious innocence;
And,—victim,—to turn executioner
Also—that feat effected, forky tongue
Had done indeed its office! Once snake's 'mouth'
Thus 'open'—how could mortal 'stop it'?"

"So!"

A tiger-flash—yell, spring, and scream: halloo!
Death 's out and on him, has and holds him—ugh!
But ne trucidet coram populo
Juvenis senem! Right the Horatian rule!

There, see how soon a quiet comes to pass!

VIII

The youth is somehow by the lady's side.
His right-hand grasps her right-hand once again.
Both gaze on the dead body. Hers the word.

"And that was good but useless. Had I lived,
The danger was to dread: but, dying now—
Himself would hardly become talkative,
Since talk no more means torture. Fools—what fools

These wicked men are! Had I borne four years,
Four years of weeks and months and days and nights,
Inured me to the consciousness of life
Coiled round by his life, with the tongue to ply,—
But that I bore about me, for prompt use
At urgent need, the thing that 'stops the mouth'
And stays the venom? Since such need was now
Or never,—how should use not follow need?
Bear witness for me, I withdraw from life
By virtue of the license—warrant, say,
That blackens yet this Album—white again,
Thanks still to my one friend who tears the page!
Now, let me write the line of supplement,
As counselled by my foe there: 'each a line!'"

And she does falteringly write to end.

"I die now through the villain who lies dead,
Righteously slain. He would have outraged me,
So, my defender slew him. God protect
The right! Where wrong lay, I bear witness now.
Let man believe me, whose last breath is spent
In blessing my defender from my soul!"

And so ends the Inn Album.

As she dies,
Begins outside a voice that sounds like song,
And is indeed half song though meant for speech
Muttered in time to motion—stir of heart
That unsubduably must bubble forth
To match the fawn-step as it mounts the stair.

"All 's ended and all 's over! Verdict found
'Not guilty'—prisoner forthwith set free,
'Mid cheers the Court pretends to disregard!
Now Portia, now for Daniel, late severe.
At last appeased, benignant! 'This young man—
Hem—has the young man's foibles but no fault.
He 's virgin soil—a friend must cultivate.
I think no plant called "love" grows wild—a friend
May introduce, and name the bloom, the fruit!'
Here somebody dares wave a handkerchief—
She 'll want to hide her face with presently!
Good-by then! 'Cigno fedel, cigno fedel,
Addio!' Now, was ever such mistake—
Ever such foolish ugly omen? Pshaw!
Wagner, beside! 'Amo te solo, te

Solo amai!' That 's worth fifty such!
But, mum, the grave face at the opened door!"

And so the good gay girl, with eyes and cheeks
Diamond and damask,—cheeks so white erewhile
Because of a vague fancy, idle fear
Chased on reflection!—pausing, taps discreet;
And then, to give herself a countenance,
Before she comes upon the pair inside,
Loud—the oft-quoted, long-laughed-over line—
"'Hail, calm acclivity, salubrious spot!'
Open the door!"

No: let the curtain fall!

Robert Browning – A Short Biography

He is the equal of any Victorian Poet that could be mentioned. However, Browning continues to be in the shadow of Tennyson, Arnold, Hopkins, Morris and many others.

Robert Browning was born on May 7th, 1812 in Walworth in the parish of Camberwell, London. He was baptized on June 14th, 1812, at Lock's Fields Independent Chapel, York Street, Walworth.

Browning's early years were certainly very interesting. His mother was an excellent pianist and a very devout evangelical Christian. His father, who worked as a clerk at the Bank of England, was also an artist, scholar, antiquarian, and collector of books and pictures. Indeed, he amassed more than 6,000 volumes of rare books including works in Greek, Hebrew, Latin, French, Italian, and Spanish. For the young and curious Browning, it was a wonderful resource, added to which his father was a guiding force in his education.

Many accounts attest that Browning was already proficient at reading and writing by the age of five. He is said to have been a bright but anxious student and to have studied and learnt Latin, Greek, and French by the time he was fourteen. From fourteen to sixteen he was educated at home, tutored in music, drawing, dancing, and horsemanship. Certainly, language and the arts were two areas the young Browning both absorbed and pushed himself towards.

At the age of twelve he wrote a volume of Byronic verse he called Incondita, which his parents attempted to have published. The attempts were unsuccessful and, disappointed, Browning destroyed the work.

In 1825, a cousin gave Browning a collection of Percy Bysshe Shelley's poetry; Browning was so enamored with the poems that he asked for the rest of Shelley's works for his thirteenth birthday. In fact, Browning then went the extra mile, declaring himself to be both a vegetarian and an atheist in honour of his hero.

Intriguingly it seems that the rejection of his first volume didn't dim his appreciation of other poets, but it appears to have stopped him writing any poems between the ages of thirteen and twenty.

In 1828, Browning enrolled at the newly-opened University of London. He was uncomfortable with the experience and he soon left, anxious to read and absorb at his own pace.

His education which, overall is notably rambling and lacks a structure that many of his artistic contemporaries enjoyed, i.e. excellent public schooling and then a degree at Oxford or Cambridge, may present many of his critics with ammunition to criticize, but alternatively his hap-hazard education certainly contributed to many of the references that baffled both critics and his audience, but they tellingly show the breath and scale of what he could turn words too. What others would call obscure references were, to Browning, remarkably obvious.

Browning's early career was very promising. His long poem Pauline (of which only a fragment was ever finished and published) brought him to the attention of the Pre-Raphaelite master Dante Gabriel Rossetti and his difficult Paracelsus (published in 1835) was warmly admired by both Dickens and Wordsworth.

In the 1830s he met the actor William Macready and was encouraged to develop and turn his talents to the stage by writing verse drama. But these plays, including Strafford, which ran for five nights in 1837, and those contained within the Bells and Pomegranates series, were, for the most part, unsuccessful.

During this period Browning began to discover that his real talents lay in taking a single character and allowing that character to discover more about himself by revealing further personal aspects of himself in his speeches; the dramatic monologue. The techniques he developed through this—especially the use of diction, rhythm, and symbol—are regarded as his most important contribution to poetry. They would later influence such major poets of the 20th Century as Ezra Pound, T. S. Eliot, and Robert Frost.

By 1840, with the publication of Sordello, the tide turned somewhat. Many thought he was being deliberately obscure, opaque beyond measure and his poetry for the next decade or so was not eagerly acquired or talked about.

As Browning attempted to rehabilitate his career he began a relationship with Elizabeth Barrett in 1845. He had read her poems and, being totally charmed by their quality, was determined to meet her. The poetess was better known than the younger Browning but suffered from a debilitating illness and was also subject to the harsh behaviour of her over-bearing father. Nevertheless, the new couple were soon inseparable.

Her father, as he did with any of his children that married, disinherited her. Despite this she had some money from her own resources and sensing that the best outcome for both the relationship and her own health was to move abroad the couple did just that. After a private marriage at St Marylebone Parish Church, in September 1846, they journeyed to Europe to honeymoon in Paris.

Their new life now took them to Italy, first to Pisa and a little later to Florence. There they absorbed life and one another.

But in the short term the literary assault on Browning's work did not let up. He was now criticized by such patrician writers as Charles Kingsley for his abandonment of England for foreign lands. Browning could do little to answer these attacks except to compose with his pen and continue with his poetical journey.

The Browning's were well respected, and even famous. Elizabeth health began to improve, she grew stronger and in 1849, at the age of 43, between four miscarriages, she gave birth to a son, Robert Wiedeman Barrett Browning, whom they nicknamed "Penini" or "Pen",

Intriguingly despite his growing reputation and return to form as a poet he was more often than not known as 'Elizabeth Barrett's husband'.

Work flowed from his pen that was to ensure his reputation as one of England's leading poets. When his collection Men and Women was published in 1855 it contained some of his finest lines. It was dedicated to Elizabeth. Life had begun to smile handsome rewards upon the Brownings.

Victorian society was very much taken with all things spiritualist. It was not enough to have command of much of the globe through Empire, they wished to know and explore wherever they could. The spirit world beckoned their interest. Browning dissented from this view believing it was all a hoax and a fraud. Elizabeth, however, was inclined to believe and this caused several disagreements between the couple.

They attended a séance by Daniel Dunglas Home, in July 1855. (Home was a famous and clamored after Scottish physical medium with the reported ability to levitate and speak with the dead). It is said that during this séance a spirit face materialised. Home then claimed it was the face of Browning's son who had died in infancy. Browning seized the 'materialisation' which turned out to be Home's bare foot. Browning had never lost a son in infancy.

After the séance, Browning wrote an angry letter to The Times, in which he said: "the whole display of hands, spirit utterances etc., was a cheat and imposture."

The Browning's time in Italy were immensely rewarding years for both their personal and professional lives. Browning encouraged her to include Sonnets from the Portuguese in her published works, these beautiful poems are undoubtedly one of the highlights of English love poetry.

Elizabeth had become quite politicised during these years. Engrossed in Italian politics (which was continuing to slowly re-unify the country), she issued a small volume of political poems entitled Poems before Congress (1860) most of which were written to express her sympathy with the Italian cause after the earlier outbreak of The Second Italian Independence War in 1859. In England they caused uproar. Conservative magazines such as Blackwood's and the Saturday Review labelled her a fanatic. She dedicated the book to her husband.

But in 1861 tragedy struck.

The couple had spent the winter of 1860–61 in Rome when Elizabeth's health deteriorated again and they returned to Florence in early June. However, these turned out to be her final weeks. Only morphine would now still the pain. She died in Browning's arms on June 29th, 1861. Browning said that she died "smilingly, happily, and with a face like a girl's .... Her last word was .... "Beautiful".

Her burial took place in the nearby Protestant English Cemetery of Florence. The local people were deeply saddened, and shops closed their doors in grief and respect.

Browning and their son were obviously devastated. Unable to bear being in Florence without Elizabeth they soon returned to London to live at 19 Warwick Crescent, Maida Vale.

As he re-integrated himself back into the London literary scene he began to finally receive the proper praise, respect and reputation that his works deserved.

Browning went on to publish Dramatis Personæ (1864), and The Ring and the Book (1868–1869). The latter, based on an "old yellow book" which told of a seventeenth-century Italian murder trial, received wide and generous critical acclaim. Although by now he was in the twilight of a long and prolific career, that had achieved some notable ups and downs, he was respected and indeed renowned for his talents and works.

In 1878, he revisited Italy for the first time since Elizabeth's death. He would return there on several further occasions but never to Florence.

Such was the esteem he was held in that The Browning Society was founded in 1881. Although he had never obtained a degree (something that set him apart from many other Victorian poets) he was now awarded honorary degrees from Oxford University in 1882 and then the University of Edinburgh in 1884.

In 1887, Browning produced the major work of his later years, Parleyings with Certain People of Importance in Their Day. Browning now spoke with his own voice as he engaged in a series of dialogues with long-forgotten figures of literary, artistic, and philosophic history. Unfortunately, both the critics and public were completely baffled by this.

On April 7th, 1889 Browning attended a dinner party at the home of his friend, the artist Rudolf Lehmann. The highlight of which was a recording made on a wax cylinder on an Edison cylinder phonograph. On the recording, which still exists, Browning recites part of How They Brought the Good News from Ghent to Aix, and can even be heard apologising when he forgets the words.

The recording was first played in 1890 on the anniversary of his death, at a gathering of his admirers, it was said to be the first time anyone's voice 'had been heard from beyond the grave'.

His last work Asolando: Fancies and Facts (1889), returned to his brief and concise lyric verse that was so popular. It was published on the day of his death on December 12th, 1889, Robert Browning was at his son's home Ca' Rezzonico in Venice.

He was buried in Poets' Corner in Westminster Abbey; his grave lies immediately adjacent to that of Alfred Tennyson.

Among the many who have publicly acknowledged their literary debt to him are Henry James, Oscar Wilde, George Bernard Shaw, G. K. Chesterton, Ezra Pound, Jorge Luis Borges, and Vladimir Nabokov.

Here follows a list of the plays and poetry volumes published during his lifetime. Poems of particular worth are noted from within those volumes.

Pauline: A Fragment of a Confession (1833)
Paracelsus (1835)
Strafford (play) (1837)
Sordello (1840)
Bells and Pomegranates No. I: Pippa Passes (play) (1841)
>	*The Year's at the Spring*
Bells and Pomegranates No. II: King Victor and King Charles (play) (1842)
Bells and Pomegranates No. III: Dramatic Lyrics (1842)
>	*Porphyria's Lover*
>	*Soliloquy of the Spanish Cloister*
>	*My Last Duchess*
>	*The Pied Piper of Hamelin*
>	*Count Gismond*
>	*Johannes Agricola in Meditation*
Bells and Pomegranates No. IV: The Return of the Druses (play) (1843)
Bells and Pomegranates No. V: A Blot in the 'Scutcheon (play) (1843)
Bells and Pomegranates No. VI: Colombe's Birthday (play) (1844)
Bells and Pomegranates No. VII: Dramatic Romances and Lyrics (1845)
>	*The Laboratory*
>	*How They Brought the Good News from Ghent to Aix*
>	*The Bishop Orders His Tomb at Saint Praxed's Church*
>	*The Lost Leader*
>	*Home Thoughts from Abroad*
>	*Meeting at Night*
Bells and Pomegranates No. VIII: Luria and A Soul's Tragedy (plays) (1846)
Christmas-Eve and Easter-Day (1850)
An Essay on Percy Bysshe Shelley (essay) (1852)
Two Poems (1854)
Men and Women (1855)
>	*Love Among the Ruins*
>	*A Toccata of Galuppi's*
>	*Childe Roland to the Dark Tower Came*
>	*Fra Lippo Lippi*
>	*Andrea Del Sarto*
>	*The Patriot*
>	*The Last Ride Together*
>	*Memorabilia*
>	*Cleon*
>	*How It Strikes a Contemporary*
>	*The Statue and the Bust*
>	*A Grammarian's Funeral*
>	*An Epistle Containing the Strange Medical Experience of Karshish, the Arab Physician*
>	*Bishop Blougram's Apology*
>	*Master Hugues of Saxe-Gotha*
>	*By the Fire-side*

Dramatis Personae (1864)
    Caliban upon Setebos
    Rabbi Ben Ezra
    Abt Vogler
    Mr. Sludge, "The Medium"
    Prospice
    A Death in the Desert
The Ring and the Book (1868–69)
Balaustion's Adventure (1871)
Prince Hohenstiel-Schwangau, Saviour of Society (1871)
Fifine at the Fair (1872)
Red Cotton Night-Cap Country, or, Turf and Towers (1873)
Aristophanes' Apology (1875)
    Thamuris Marching
The Inn Album (1875)
Pacchiarotto, and How He Worked in Distemper (1876)
    Numpholeptos
The Agamemnon of Aeschylus (1877)
La Saisiaz and The Two Poets of Croisic (1878)
Dramatic Idylls (1879)
Dramatic Idylls: Second Series (1880)
    Pan and Luna
Jocoseria (1883)
Ferishtah's Fancies (1884)
Parleyings with Certain People of Importance in Their Day (1887)
Asolando (1889)
    Prologue
    Summum Bonum
    Bad Dreams III
    Flute-Music, with an Accompaniment
    Epilogue

www.ingramcontent.com/pod-product-compliance
Lightning Source LLC
Chambersburg PA
CBHW060144050426
42448CB00010B/2285